THE B.S.
BEHIND THE BADGE

And The Courage to Wear it With Honor

ISBN: 0996573003
ISBN 13: 9780996573009

A portion of the proceeds from sales of *The B.S. Behind the Badge and the Courage to Wear it with Honor* go to the California Narcotic Officers' Association Survivor's Memorial Fund (CNOA/SMF). Unforeseen expenses always result when a law enforcement officer suddenly dies. This nonprofit group assists the families of California police officers killed in the line of duty.

Introduction

Few jobs have the bullshit that cops have to put up with. From political agendas, legislative mandates, and public opinion to being spit at, shot at, and killed, peace officers unselfishly put their lives on the line to maintain a quality of life for our country that decent people appreciate. I have been privileged to serve in such a capacity and luckily am able to share my observations in this book, with particular comment on the de-emphasis of enforcing laws such as narcotic violations, public behavior, and other violent crimes that are resurfacing to plague our communities. Policing is like insurance: we want it, we need it, and we pay the premiums. When it is used only in emergencies and viewed as unnecessary, people want it cheaper or not at all. When a tragedy strikes, they regret the day they cancelled it. I offer here a behind-the-scenes view of police work, based on three decades of experience as first a local police officer and then as a state special agent with the California Department of Justice.

The State of California's Department of Justice had a law enforcement section known to many in the law enforcement industry. Those that have been in the profession of narcotic law enforcement knew us as the "State Narcs," while our official title was the

Bureau of Narcotic Enforcement (BNE). The BNE was established in 1927 and was the nation's oldest narcotic enforcement unit. This dedicated group of peace officers were called Special Agents, and they were an exceptional breed of cop. These Special Agents worked undercover, carried firearms, worked long and unusual hours, and were seasoned investigators with various areas of expertise, including undercover operations, major investigations, and tracking down criminals. They had statewide jurisdiction to conduct criminal investigations; make arrests; seize evidence; and file criminal cases with local, state, and federal prosecutors.

BNE Special Agents worked with police departments and other state and federal agencies throughout the country. Agencies like LAPD, LASD, CHP, BATF, DEA, FBI, and U.S. Marshals, to name a few, have been partners in this endeavor. With a rich history and evolution, BNE had become California's leader in narcotic enforcement. However, due to political and economic climates, BNE was dismantled in 2012 and other police agencies were forced to reorganize and downsize their narcotic and specialized units that target major crime.

It's the cops who arrest, enforce, and keep the peace out there in our streets. They fight with desperate criminals in dark alleys and routinely get wounded, emotionally scarred, and worse. They act as family counselor, doctor, financial advisor, lawyer, social worker, and psychiatrist. They also break up gang fights, are thrown into raging gun battles, conduct high-speed pursuits, and are expected to maintain courageous calm with perfect decision making. They've missed their kid's soccer games and back-to-school nights, and they have worked every holiday while others were closed for business and at home with their families. This is not the job for someone who wants banker's hours. But police officers choose this life because they want to make everyone's life a little safer and a little better, not just their own.

We as a society kept our eye on the ball. That's why crime rates over the past several years have been going down. Now the emphasis has changed as budgets have shrunk and the political will to do the right thing has fatigued. Holding the career criminal/drug addict/drug dealer accountable is not the approach society wants to take any more. Politics and lawsuits—along with the sudden national priority of cigarette tax stamp evasion, environmental crimes, and the mortgage crisis—have blurred society's view of what an effective, professional and compassionate police force should do.

Thus, society has re-evaluated its need for "insurance" (the police).

The early release of convicted felons per the new California state law AB 109 (prison overcrowding) and California State proposition 47 (downgrades narcotic felonies and the three strikes law) has exacerbated the hit to the criminal justice system. Crimes like burglary and narcotic offenses were suddenly deemed not worthy of state prison sentences. DNA swabs are no longer conducted on these felons. Many crimes committed in the past by a repeat offender can be solved today since the technology now exists to use DNA evidence that was obtained through a swab. But these cases will be missed now. Also some are exonerated by DNA. The courts used to mandate intervention to help a drug addict kick the habit when they were involved in felony crimes, but they will no longer do so since what used to be a felony crime has been stricken from the books.

Society has the absolute right to govern and evaluate its laws and policing. Sometimes society is right but sometimes it is wrong. We now are experiencing a dramatic uptick in violent assaults on both police officers and the public, property crimes, and the burdening of local law enforcement with parole duties. We are also seeing an epidemic horror of drug use as legalization experiments are played out in our country. No doubt these laws will be revisited by the voters and the legislature when the boiling point returns. My personal opinion is that the boiling point has already arrived.

We've taken our eye off the ball.

Police work has suffered a blow with scandals and funding. It is difficult to recruit and retain qualified personnel to do, without argument, the toughest job around. It is also the most satisfying and rewarding experience one could have. I have been fortunate to work alongside some of the best and bravest people I have ever known. They have an incredible sense of duty, honor, and willingness to help others, even at their own peril. Society waxes and wanes with its views towards police. One such view, the "War on Drugs" as it is incorrectly referred to, is not a war; rather, it is a national debate of a civilized society in the best country in the world trying to grapple with what it wants to allow as a freedom or a criminal act. The debate rages on.

Society will crucify a cop who had milliseconds to make a life-or-death decision, but others will get a pass because they are famous or represent a minority. Do we really need lectures from our leaders that plastic bags are dangerous to the environment along with fast food and "big gulps" being criminal? We enact laws to protect us from the "ferocious" 32-ounce cola but think it's ok to release hardened criminals from prison because a non-violent felony crime landed them there? Trust me, I've seen many trials and you have to be quite the over-achiever to land in state prison. News flash: you don't go to prison for smoking pot.

I am neither a Rhodes Scholar nor a member of a think tank. I know we will never eradicate drugs; it is far too late for that. What we can do is ***limit*** the poison, death, and misery drug use wreaks upon our society. This book gives a perspective from being in a line of work like no other, one that acutely exposes the human condition in relation to liberty and justice. No one wants to live in an intoxicated society with criminals roaming free or in a police state with our freedoms trampled upon. We live in an amazing country. It's not perfect, and cops aren't perfect, but both are worth fighting for.

DEDICATION: To my amazing wife and kids who are the best human beings I have ever known. They put up with the long hours, the emotional roller coasters, and the empty seat at the dinner table. Their love, courage and support gives me strength to stay focused on the real goals of law enforcement, which is to make our cities a little safer, bring criminals to justice, and to protect those who cannot protect themselves. And to my parents, along with my brother, and sister who are the core of what's right in the world. Last but not least, to those who have sacrificed their lives in keeping the peace: my fellow cops who truly are the unsung heroes that keep society from falling into the abyss.

Table of Contents

1

Initiation

*"We sleep safely at night because rough men stand
ready to visit violence on those who would harm us".*

— WINSTON CHURCHILL

In 1984, with college degree in hand, I started my law enforcement career as a police officer for the city of Glendale, California. I applied for the job along with 300 other applicants. Only five positions were being filled. These were coveted jobs back then, as they still are now. Firefighter and police careers were always lined with thousands of applicants. Before "Best Buy" and "Target" had their Black Friday sales attracting half a city's population to their stores, you would have the same amount of people lining up around city blocks just for the opportunity to test for a handful of these civil service careers. It was a much sought after job and frankly the hiring requirements were much more stringent back then. Psychological, physical, medical, and intellectual tests as well as an in-depth background check were conducted and evaluated like no other line of work out there.

The final portion of the process involved an extensive background investigation where I was placed under a microscope. Every aspect of my life was checked; people who knew me both past and present were interviewed, including teachers, employers, friends, relatives, neighbors; school records were reviewed. No stone was left unturned. Everyone I ever knew or had contact with was interviewed. They did this to obtain a clear picture of the applicant—namely, me. It is this phase of the hiring process that usually washed out the majority of applicants, especially when it came to drug use.

In addition to the calling of this type of job, I was young and did not think of retirement planning or 401(k)'s. I just wanted to work in job that I knew would be challenging and enjoyable, and in which I knew I could make a difference. Only as I continued into my career did I come to realize the absolute satisfaction of a rewarding career and the solace of a defined benefit plan that awaited me if I ran the course and lived to tell about it. Crossing that finish line is quite a feeling, as many of my coworkers had died in the line of duty or had their careers cut short due to illness, self- destruction, or suicide. Some died right after their retirement, never living long enough to even collect a few years pension after putting in 30-plus years as a first responder. Crossing that finish line is only half the prize; the other half was making a liar out of the pension system who banks on us living 10 years less than the average American male. Most actuary tables have law enforcement personnel dying a few years after retirement[i].

Over the years, I have had conversations with my private sector friends and some of them truly felt the retirement pension was an unfair "gift" to law enforcement. Why should we be granted a pension when they don't have one? There are also some legislators that feel this way and try to propose legislation to minimize the benefits of law enforcement officers. Some of these people make significantly more money than the average cop. On the other hand, most police pensions do not pay into social security so we are unable to draw from that public benefit. Well, I say to all: try walking a mile in a cop's shoes. If they can make the grade and pass, endure all the ongoing training and stress, and face the life-and-death issues that only come with this career, then we can talk. It's called a safety retirement for a reason.

So too does our military deserve such pensions. America recently saw, in the VA scandals of 2013 and 2014, some veterans who died waiting for medical care in this country. This is absolutely inexcusable. That said, cops and military are identical in that they put their lives on the line, for total strangers, and they don't make millions while doing it like professional athletes, legislators, celebrities, or corporate executives often do. Police pensions are modest in comparison to these professions. I do not fault or criticize those people for making money. I know I could have stood in that line, but no regrets, I'm glad I stood in the other.

Who do all those people call if they are suddenly victims of a crime or need help? I think you know. Yes, private sector gets pink-slipped if the boss doesn't like them and cops enjoy a certain level of civil service protections. This is because a law enforcement career is infinitely more complex and demanding than any of the previously mentioned careers. That's not meant to insult anybody, that's just a fact. If that corporate VP has his or her house broken into, do they pick up the phone and call 911 so a fellow business partner can help them deal with the 6'2" parolee who just cut his ankle bracelet and is now standing in their kid's bedroom? No. The law enforcement professional has an infinitely greater responsibility to the public and to their fellow citizens. Like our military brethren, we actually count the days we have left in our career from the day we start, since getting out alive to enjoy the rest of our life is the goal and not one easily attained.

Getting back to the hiring process, then, the requirement was no hard drug use EVER. Can you imagine that standard being applied to today's population? In addition, if marijuana was used, it had to have happened at least *one decade* before you applied for the job as a cop. Even then, if it came down to two qualified applicants and one had tried or "just inhaled" marijuana and the other had not experimented with it, guess who didn't get the job? Today this standard would be impossible to implement. The majority of the candidate pool in this generation would be eliminated from the process. Then, it was an automatic disqualifier. Today, it is typically mitigated. This is not to say I or any other applicant at that time were choir boys, this was just a statement of our times and the cops reflected the population that it served.

Today and in recent years, more of our population has tried drugs, even hard drugs, especially during their high school and college years. Some committed low-level crimes or came from troubled homes. It doesn't make them bad people; it just makes them human.

It's what they made of themselves afterwards that shows their character. Did they learn from their mistakes, get good grades in school, and live a quality life to be a cop worthy of the public's trust and honorable enough to swear an oath to protect the innocent and enforce our laws?

Remember that after the initial tests and questions for hiring came the background investigation. This usually revealed the use of drugs, even if the applicant had lied about it. Of course, if the applicant had snorted cocaine or smoked a joint a few days before applying (and this has happened) of course he or she would not go further in the selection process. This standard has since been revisited in order to allow the police officer candidate pool to expand and truly reflect the population it serves. The days of little or no drug use by our country's population are gone.

Cultural changes have affected the hiring process too. The all-white police forces from the past decades have started to change and reflect a more diverse population and an Americanized one as more immigrants assimilate to our country's way of life. This is a slow change across the United States and is a work in progress. Some cultures and heritages, including my own, have stigmas associated with being a cop. That will take more time to completely overcome as foreign cultures and some American minorities still struggle with the perception of policing in America. The premise that only minority officers can police minority communities is in and of itself racist, as is the idea that minority politicians can only govern minority communities. Also, cities that have a majority of one race or another as its base population are striving to have its police force integrated but that too will take more time. And consider pay and locality issues: it's challenging to get someone to move to a high-cost or high-crime area like Southern California or New York to work in a job like this. It is a rewarding career, but it is not for the faint of heart.

Back to me. After several months of written testing, interviews, physical exams, psychological exams, and the full background investigation, I made the cut. I and the other lucky candidates were given job offers and went to the Police Academy at the Los Angeles County Sheriff's Department. For 19 weeks I was pushed to my limits both physically and mentally. I was young and single at the time, so I devoted 100 percent to the job. This was a once-in-a-lifetime experience for me that I can't put into words.

Several of the local police departments contracted with the Sheriff's Academy to train their new officers alongside the sheriff's deputies. This was a great way to drive the point home that we were all in this together, regardless of sex, race, religion, or what law enforcement agency badge we wore. No racial tensions, no discrimination—just a blend of society's best and bravest men and women. We started with 130 cadets and graduated with just over 100. Throughout the 19 weeks, several cadets were fired, asked to resign, or simply quit on their own.

I remember one fellow cadet who was in my platoon. We had just completed our firearms training and what was one of the most philosophical and thought-provoking classes I have ever taken in my life. I've had college courses in psychology and a lifetime of theological courses from being raised Catholic. This particular class, though, was regarding the use of deadly force. One of the topics for discussion was if we, as human beings, could take another's life to defend the public or oneself. Scenarios were discussed and debated. Many of our group had never really considered this possibility, even though we all knew it was a reality in this job. I had a very moving conversation with this other cadet who came to the realization that he could not bring himself to kill a human being, regardless of the circumstance. The next day he resigned. I respected and admired him for his beliefs. It took courage for him to face such an issue knowing that in the greater good, should he have been in such a circumstance in his career, the lives of others would be on the line.

This type of situation is just one of a myriad of the complexities that police work carries. The academy training was, without a doubt, the most challenging experience I had ever undertaken at that point in my life. The sense of accomplishment in completing this first phase of a cop's career was indescribable. I was in the best shape of my life and wanted to prove my skills when I swore an oath to protect those who could not protect themselves.

I will share a few experiences from those early days working the streets, where I saw firsthand how society languishes with its criminals and drug problem.

Once I graduated from the Police Academy, I was immediately assigned to a field training officer (FTO) in the patrol division. After a brief time of orientation to the various functions within the police department, we hit the streets as a patrol unit. The next benchmark for me was every rookie officer's goal: the time to be the driver instead of the "bookman."

Otherwise known as riding shotgun, the bookman typically handled the radio, reports, and the map book of the city. This was in the days before smart phones and GPS mapping devices you could plug into the cigarette adapter. The FTO was the driver and had the job of showing the rookie (me) how to be a good cop. We handled the usual calls like family disturbances,

911 calls, and traffic accidents; wrote tickets; responded to silent bank robbery alarms or burglaries in progress and reports of runaways, just to name a few of our duties. I was exposed to the typical calls for service that the public pays for its officers to handle. More importantly, my FTO taught me the proactive approach. This skill is the honed instinct that cops use every day to prevent crime and truly protect our communities. Making self-initiated quality arrests by developing lawful probable cause then conducting solid field investigations, solving crimes, helping others and taking the bad guy off the street is the satisfaction any good cop strives for.

Well, after just a few weeks I got my wish. As my FTO and I left the station after our daily roll call briefing, I was accustomed to walking toward the passenger side of the car and then loading up the Ithaca 12 gauge shotgun and placing it in the shotgun rack. He must have lagged behind because he was about 20 feet behind me when I got to our car. I turned to look back at him, wondering why he was so far back. He just looked at me and said "Here you go." He tossed me the keys to the black and white (patrol car). I felt like a wide receiver catching a touchdown pass at the Super Bowl. I made the catch; composed myself, got into the driver's seat, and off we went into the night.

The next milestone for a new cop is when you're on your own and your FTO kicks you out of the nest as a "one man car," or "L" car. Two months later this came to pass for me. This was the time for me to apply the skills I had learned both in the academy and on the various calls I had responded to and most importantly the experience gained from working with my FTO. I was a sponge and had absorbed the spectrum thrown at me in these early months.

I cannot emphasize enough how critical the guidance of the FTO is to the baseline training. He acted as if every moment of his job was being nationally televised and he was a role model who led by example. He taught me lessons that have stayed with me throughout my law enforcement career. Thank you, Randy O.

I worked the usual shifts: days, swing shift, PMs, overlap, and graveyard. The police culture is a unique one. Like in the military, a certain bonding happens when people work together, face adversity and achieve victories together, and come to know the stress of life-and-death issues that are part of the job together. This is the backbone of the police service. Every range of the human condition is dealt with. By working all hours of the day and night, a complete perspective of society can be seen.

I was able to truly see how the world works, at both its best and its worst. This experience is invaluable, especially when it comes to leading a law enforcement agency or managing specialized units such as a narcotic unit. By virtue of working patrol, certain skills are taught and reinforced that serve as a foundation to build on.

Take, for example, the relatively simple call to a traffic accident. Information must be collected, witnesses interviewed, evidence collected, and an arrest might be made such as in the case of a drunk driver. Tensions are high when dealing with people who are in a hysterical or injured condition. The exposure to dynamic thinking and being professional under stressful conditions is tested at this level of police work: patrol work. The radio calls of a "211 in progress" (a robbery), "Baby not breathing," and "Shots fired, officer needs help" make a patrol officer's adrenaline burst through the roof.

If one does not have the discipline or maturity to handle this emotion and arrive at the scene safely and in time to make a difference, the cop will have a short career and others could be hurt. I was fortunate to have solid training and the common sense to deal with these types of situations. Also it was important to be surrounded by peers who were compassionate human beings, willing to sacrifice themselves for others to keep the peace.

I have always kept an open mind, and as I continued to work the various shifts, I quickly learned the reality that the public and the criminal share the same society.

Being a one-man unit offers a great feeling of accomplishment, but having a partner by your side is tactically the best strategy. There was a concept of policing in the early 1980s that made the public think there were more cops on the street. Back then, as now, fiscal and political issues faced all California police departments. Other than when in training or in a specialized unit, two-man cars used to be the norm. There was much heated debate over splitting up a two-man patrol car team, but virtually overnight, one-man cars became fashionable. This was done to save money and to stretch the dollar as far as it could go.

Consider this example: say **four** "black and whites" (police cars) were assigned to an area with two cops in each car. You had eight cops to address any problem that came up. Your backup officer was right next to you, in the passenger seat. This simple two-man presence went a long way in handling disturbances, bar fights, crimes in progress, foot pursuits, and angry people who thought twice about spitting on or picking a fight with a police officer.

Then the two-man cars became one-man cars. Well, imagine the delight of the public when they saw **eight** black and whites out there instead of **four**. The public felt their police department had doubled their patrols with *16* police officers on the streets. The public thought twice as many cops were patrolling the city. This was an incredible PR move in the mind of the police executives and city bureaucrats who implemented it. In reality, it was the same number of cops—*eight* of them—only now they were spread out and spread thin. It looked great to the public, and economics supported this new wave of policing.

This type of strategy is done by many law enforcement agencies trying to have a more visible presence with what they have and to justify practices to funding and public demands. The downfall was that the traditional partner concept was broken up and each police officer is left alone in the car. This diluting effect eroded the officer safety concept and took away the valuable tool of having instant backup, as well as another set of eyes to help see trouble and minimize violent contact with the public.

Officers have developed an individualistic attitude and the "tombstone courage" syndrome was a side effect. Tombstone courage is when a lone officer feels he can truly do it all by himself, which sometimes includes facing a deadly confrontation due to a false sense of bravado. This usually results in the death of the officer, hence the tombstone reference. Yes, this does build a self-reliant officer, but it also inhibits the proactive approach and gets a lot of cops hurt or killed. A frightened citizen may call the police department to report a suspicious person who does not live in the area, who is out at 3:00 a.m. walking through a residential neighborhood, staring through the windows of houses as he walks by. The public demands a good cop to investigate. I don't care the color of their skin, what religion they profess, or if they just wanted to get some air. That individual should be professionally contacted and rightfully so.

A two-man car obviously has the tactical advantage when contacting the reported individual. One officer would start the usual questioning and the other would be vigilantly studying the person's body language or at least visually searching for signs of concealed weapons or intoxication. If this person suddenly fled or became combative, two on one is much better odds for capture. A potentially hazardous situation is dealt with efficiently and safely. Minimal force is used because two people are working together and have already rehearsed or experienced similar types of encounters.

A solo officer should not contact such a person until backup has arrived or is nearby. Unfortunately this is now a luxury and today, that solo officer has to make that contact alone most of the time. If the suspect is combative or actively casing homes to commit a burglary, rape, or other crime, a single officer offers a 50/50 chance to the criminal to fight or escape. Good odds if you are a bad guy.

There exist numerous horror stories of cops being killed in the line of duty because they were alone. For example, a Riverside deputy sheriff was killed by a man during a "routine" disturbance call. Let me say this: there is nothing *routine* about police work. In this case, the deputy sheriff was a solo patrol officer who responded to the call and was immediately engaged in a struggle with the suspect. The officer, Deputy Lee, was beaten and unconscious by the time backup arrived.[ii]

Should a fight or pursuit ensue on any call, a solo officer has to overcome resistance with more vigor because he or she is alone and has a real potential of being hurt or letting the suspect get away. I would bet there has been an increase in excessive use of force complaints as a result of this necessary vigor by a solo officer. The officer's word against the suspect's word used to be a non-issue. The cop was always right and had a witness (his backup) to prove it. Today that is not true. Scandals and lawsuits have tipped the scales in favor of the suspect. The public is now cynical of law enforcement. A second officer could greatly reduce the anxiety felt during these types of contacts and actually lower the liability risk. A recording of the event could also address any wrongdoing done by the officer or citizen.

I'm sure you can see where I am going with this. Leave the pair of officers intact. If the community is paying for two officers, keep them together. It might cost more, but it is an investment (insurance) that pays off in dividends. It ensures a better quality of service, adds a deterring factor to criminals, lowers citizen complaints, and maintains an acceptable level of officer and citizen safety, rather than spreading the thin blue line even thinner.

Getting back to shift work, I was alone—a one-man car, working the most unnatural shift, graveyard shift, or "graves". It actually is a fun shift for a cop since the general public is not there to interfere with the customary PR (public relations) calls that routinely happen. Every contact I made in a patrol stop seemed to result in an arrest or a good field interview card. Some officers loved working these hours, and I did too, to a point. But I felt like a vampire: awake all night then sleeping all day. It is kind of ironic that law enforcement refers to the quiet late night and morning hour as a graveyard, but nonetheless it is true.

Everything after 0200 hours (2:00 a.m.) is eerily still. The bars close down, most businesses are closed for the night, and traffic is light. Anyone out roaming the streets or driving around aimlessly was usually up to no good. Being proactive, looking for circumstances out of place, responding to calls from the community, and putting the public safety first tempered with maintaining the constitutional rights we all have, are all effective ways to keep the peace. Following are a few of the experiences I had that illustrate these duties.

The first example occurred one morning while I was on patrol. I was being proactive, looking for anything out of place, and experienced some unexpected consequences.

It was about 3:30 a.m. and I saw a beat up, early '70s Chevrolet 4-door sedan driving northbound on Brand Boulevard. Mind you, there were no other cars on the road except us. The posted speed limit was 25 mph and he was going 15 mph. Also his right turn indicator was on but he was not turning. This is not a big crime in the scheme of things. He posed no immediate danger to any other motorists since he and I were the only ones out there. I had a bad feeling—call it instinct—but that is what motivates a good cop to be curious. These are also called clues in police work.

As I drove up from behind, I saw him checking his passenger side view mirror constantly, as if preparing for a lane change but he never turned. He passed three intersections without turning.

It was a cold morning and he had all four windows rolled down completely. Even if you are not a cop, doesn't this circumstance seem odd? Well, that was my conclusion. Again, race, sex, politics, social status, or astrological charts did not factor into my decision making. I exercised my legal authority based on training and experience to pull him over.

I more than satisfied the Probable Cause requirement needed to conduct the traffic stop based on the vehicle code violations previously mentioned. I was already evaluating the possible reasons for this driving behavior. It is normal to triage such a set of facts before making a traffic stop. The first possible reason was that he must be drunk, coming back from a party at a friend's house. His windows were probably rolled down because he was falling asleep and he wanted to stay awake to make the drive home. Sounds reasonable. The next thought I had was that maybe this guy had something in his car he wanted to protect, so he was driving excessively slow. The window thing could be due to inoperable door motors. Or worse yet, he could have just committed a murder and was leaving the scene. As you can see, a lot of possibilities exist and race through the mind of every police officer before initiating a traffic stop.

It is typical for a cop to digest these possibilities in a few precious minutes, circumstances that others might take an eternity to notice and consider. I knew based on the circumstances that this was not going to be just a routine traffic stop. Duty called and I needed to investigate further.

Enough of the guesswork, I activated my overhead light bar and gave a quick short burst of the siren. After another two long blocks, I thought I had a Failure to Yield (someone not willing to pull over), so anticipating a pursuit, I gave him another chance to comply by picking up the mike (microphone) to use the PA (public address system) and ordering him to pull to the curb. He finally realized I was behind him and pulled over. I exited my patrol car and as I approached the driver's side of the door, I looked at him: a male adult in his 20s, who had a blank stare on his face as he stared forward, both hands gripping the steering wheel like it was glued to his hands. Instantly, I smelled a strong chemical odor coming from the interior of the car. In this cold night, I had smelled this odor a few times before. It was an ether-like smell—sweet yet foul. It was the drug of the 80s, liquid PCP.

I asked him for his driver's license and he moved as if he was in a slow-motion video. He was sweating like he had just run a marathon, and I was anxiously awaiting my backup who was still a few minutes away (remember we lost the advantage of having a partner immediately available in the car). On any traffic stop, if your beat partner was not tied up on a call, he or she would always roll by to see if you were Code 4 (all secure). In this case, I had formally requested a backup before pulling to the curb as I had a feeling this would not be the typical ticket. Backup arrived while I continued the typical field investigation, which includes evaluating sobriety level and gaining more information as to why the driver is roaming the streets at such an hour.

I asked the driver to get out of the car and stand at the curb so I could perform the customary battery of field sobriety tests. He was very slow in reacting to my instruction, and then he carefully got out of the car and walked to the curb. He was unable to complete the basic "touch the tip of your nose" test as he lost his balance several times. I immediately noticed his stride when I asked him to walk a straight line for me. I thought he was imitating Neil Armstrong's moon walk.

This exaggerated walking is a classic symptom of being under the influence of PCP. This drug elevates the body's core temperature and that is the reason for the profuse sweating, even in cold weather. No wonder this guy had his windows rolled down; he was burning up!

Based on experience and training, I quickly concluded we had a duster. A duster is what we called PCP users, referring to the powdered version of the drug, which was also called Angel Dust. I immediately stopped any further DUI tests and handcuffed him before he could blink. A word of caution when dealing with persons under the influence of this drug: Loud, boisterous, quick movements can set off an individual who is calm and still somewhat coherent while under the influence of PCP. Being forceful with sudden movements or being loud or overbearing can agitate these people. Bright flashing lights can excite them and then the fight is on. As I mentioned before, one good thing that a one-man car teaches you is self-reliance and maturity. I learned to buy time and to be patient. This is one of those times in life where discretion was the better part of valor.

Prior to the vehicle being impounded, I conducted an inventory inspection of the car so the city tow truck company could be assured the car they were about to put into their tow yard was free of any weapons or contraband. As I checked the interior of the car, I noticed a shoe box on the floor behind the driver's seat. (This proved to be a bit of foreshadowing for me, as years later the shoe box would again appear in my next job as a BNE Special Agent.)

The chemical smell I noticed at the beginning of the traffic stop seemed to be coming from the box. I opened the lid of the box and noticed five small amber glass bottles labeled "Schilling vanilla flavor extract." One of these bottles was tipped over in the box and had leaked out some of its content: liquid PCP. The bottom of the shoe box was soaked with this liquid and I had held the box with my bare hands. I immediately wiped my hands on my uniform pants.

I placed the box back in the suspect's car, went to my patrol car to take out my evidence collection kit. I put the items into a plastic bag, sealed it and brought it into the station along with my prisoner for booking and post-arrest procedures.

I was writing my report at the station and had to go home two hours later due to having a severe headache. This was my first physical contact with such a chemical and I had been an unwilling victim of PCP exposure. Back in those days, cops routinely handled dangerous chemicals and drugs without gloves, or just wearing leather gloves rather than the surgical kind now readily available. We have come a long way and today you can't even book PCP evidence at police department evidence lockers since it is now considered a hazardous material.

Anyway, I arrested the suspect for possession for sales of narcotics. No single human could ingest five ounces of PCP, let alone be carrying it for personal or any legitimate medical purpose. He had enough liquid PCP or "juice" to anesthetize a city block. Those five, one-ounce bottles of PCP were the preferred method for selling and using the drug. The dealer would sell these bottles to another sub-dealer who would dip about half of a Sherman brand cigarette into the Schilling amber bottle.

The bottle was the perfect size to accommodate the thin cigarette and soak it in PCP for the user to smoke later. This is why a PCP-laced cigarette was called a "sherm." The dealer bathed the cigarette in the lethal liquid then allowed it to dry to be put into a regular cigarette box for future use. These laced cigarettes were sold individually or in a pack. Pretty ingenious at the time, since a lot of thugs smoked it back then, particularly parolees and gangsters.

It was commonplace to see a pack of cigarettes in the hands of these misguided people. If a cop was not paying attention to the other cues around them or was not properly trained, the criminal would get away with using the PCP-laced cigarettes. Worse yet, they would sell it to kids. Again, the proactive approach was needed. Of course I could not stop and frisk everyone with a pack of cigarettes. That's ridiculous. Common sense and the rule of law always should dictate an officer's decision making when initiating such contact with the public.

I will tell you this: If a group of persons were in a gang-infested, high-parolee population area with a known history of PCP sales in the neighborhood and the group was dressed like the local gangs with the shaved heads, wearing the colors of a gang, and smoking in a secluded corner of a park, a police officer would be derelict in his or her duties and would let down the community if no field investigation was made. During this time in the 1980s, police officers were still regarded in high esteem and scandals were rare.

The public largely supported their police forces. Narcotic enforcement was in its "hey day." The newspapers chronicled the crack cocaine epidemic and the Columbian cartels that had invaded U.S. soil with their product. Large multi-kilogram amounts of cocaine were routinely being seized at the border. Stash houses, where large amounts of money or narcotics were stored, were popping up all around Los Angeles County and Southern California.

Several agencies, including the Los Angeles Police Department, The Los Angeles County Sheriff's Department, BNE, FBI, and DEA, were conducting investigations into these major narcotic traffickers. The local agencies had to address the street dealer who was taking over most of their inner cities' residential neighborhoods. Orange, Riverside, and San Bernardino Counties were going through the same experience. My patrol experience exposed me to society's insatiable appetite for drugs. Patrol is the first line of defense, and next comes the detective work most cops aspire toward. As a patrol officer, I was often called upon to assist these various agencies.

Assisting an outside police agency with a search warrant service whenever they wanted to execute a warrant within our city limits was a fairly common request. Usually our Patrol Bureau handled the requests and dispatched an area patrol officer to respond. The outside agency would always call the watch commander and ask for a "black and white" to act as a uniformed presence at the front door while the plainclothes detectives served the warrant. By doing this, the drug dealers or the innocent occupants in the house would be certain that the police were lawfully demanding entry into the premises and were not a rival criminal trying to get their ill-gotten proceeds. There were times that the lawful knock-and-notice requirement needed to be given in both Spanish and English to conform to this legal requirement.

Once when I was on patrol, working a day watch, I received a dispatch to assist an LA County Sheriff's major narcotic team with the service of a search warrant. Unbeknownst to me, the team waiting for me around the corner were a different breed of cop. I met with the Sergeant and his crew for the first time and was briefed on their plan to serve the narcotic search warrant. As protocol required, they wanted a uniformed officer at the front door as they were serving the warrant.

My job was to assist with the knock-and-notice requirement and stay until they had secured the location. I gave the customary announcement, "Police, we have a search warrant. Open the door," in both Spanish and English. I repeated this command several times. When no one responded, the sheriff's narcotic team had to force the door open to gain entry.

I remained outside at the doorstep and within minutes they put out a Code 4. The Sergeant thanked me for my assistance and I left. I resumed my patrol duties and felt I had made a contribution to narcotic enforcement for the day. However, years later this same narcotic team was indicted as one of the most corrupt group of cops that ever wore the badge. They were prosecuted and ultimately incarcerated. This corruption scandal ripped through the police community, and rightfully so. There is no place for such officers, and they were brought to justice.

Another example of my patrol duties often involved violence. I sometimes felt that I should have been a professional boxer or wrestler since there is a typical police scenario that always involves fighting: a "disturbance of the peace" call. One evening I received such a call and was dispatched to "415 Man in the Alley" (section 415 of the Ca. Penal Code defines a public disturbance). It was a Friday night about 2200 hours (10:00 p.m.). Upon arrival, three units were already talking to a male adult in his 30s who was standing in a rear yard that opened up to an alley. This man appeared disoriented and was talking loudly and making no sense. The officers on the scene were trying to get him down from a roof of a "yard car" (typically an abandoned vehicle parked in the front or back yard of a residence) that was parked in the rear of the house. The yard was full of junked cars. He displayed all the objective symptoms of being under the influence of PCP. With this fact in mind, one of my partners was very astute and broadcasted over his hand-held police radio for additional backup units. He also broadcasted to have the responding units arrive "blacked out" (no lights or sirens). As the minutes dragged on and this person was not listening to our requests to come down from the roof, backup finally arrived.

Of course the responding unit was coming in a little fast (remember the adrenaline surge that must be controlled by every cop) and I could hear the squealing tires coming down the alley. I was focused on the agitated male, who at this time was trying to kick us as we got close to his feet as he stood on the roof of the car. His kicks nearly took off my head, but I was able to bob and weave, avoiding being kicked in the face. We were facing the suspect and our backs were to the alley.

The backup unit did not come in blacked out. As I heard the wail of the siren, I saw the splash of red and blue lights dancing all around us in that dark alley. The suspect froze for about a minute, fixated on the lights, literally like a deer in the headlights about to be run over. I immediately got a case of the "awshitz." My partner got on his radio and yelled into the microphone "ALL units, turn off lights and sirens when responding, we have a duster."

It was too late; the fight was on.

The suspect reacted as if he was a twisted rubber band and the tension was finally allowed to break loose. He started wildly yelling and screaming and jumping from the roof of one car to another. He even made it onto the roof of one of our patrol vehicles.

After this acrobatic maneuver, he got to the ground and stared at the five of us, four of us holding batons while the other officer had the handcuffs out, ready to cuff him. He was incoherent and beyond the point of reasoning. He raised his arms, fists clenched, and started swinging at us. A couple of swift and focused baton strikes seemed to stun him, and then all of us were on top of him, barely getting his arms behind him to cuff him. I will never forget how he felt. I was holding his right leg at the calf area and could feel his pulse through his leg. He was soaking wet from perspiration and radiated heat like a barbeque.

PCP is a particular nasty drug because there are two extremes while under its influence. You are either completely docile, open to any suggestion, and moving slowly, or you are violently combative, verbally abusive, and virtually immune to pain. Our suspect had gone from one extreme to the other.

We ended up taking him to jail and, according to witnesses, the suspect was only a casual user of PCP. I always laugh at that word, *casual*. There is nothing casual about digesting a drug with only one legitimate medical purpose—as a horse tranquilizer. Yes, a horse tranquilizer. This convict had a criminal record, a substance abuse problem, and a conviction for resisting arrest. I know, shocking huh? And yet his neighbors labeled him as a casual user. I ask anyone: Who would want this drug legalized?

After putting this drug in your system a few times, it acts much like LSD in that it is stored in the fatty tissue of the human body. That means that a user is prone to flashbacks of being under the influence, just as if he just took a new hit from a PCP-laced sherm, without actually having to ingest it. Remember, some jobs require drug screening and random testing. He would never pass such a test since it would be years before the PCP was out of his system. This onetime, probably decent man is now kept out of the majority of the job market. Who would hire a drug addicted ex- con? But users do this all for the strange joy of getting high.

Let me reiterate, PCP is a hard core drug and is illegal. One effect it has is giving one the appearance of super human strength. Documented cases have these suspects withstanding physical force applied from baton strikes, hands-on control techniques from multiple officers trying to restrain them, and multiple gunshots, and they have even been known to break a set of standard police handcuffs. Sure they were able to pull apart the cuffs that had a tensile strength of 2,200 pounds, but in the process the suspect broke each wrist. Or the suspect was able to fight with four cops and throw them around like rag dolls.

That's because PCP numbs the part of the brain that registers pain, so the super strength is really just the suspension of the body's pain signals. Cops have been killed in the line of duty by criminals under the influence of PCP. Its onetime legitimate use in the 1950s was as a horse tranquilizer. Why anyone in their wildest dreams would want to use a drug that puts to sleep a 1,000-pound animal is beyond me.

Another example of dealing with a drug user was one night in 1986, around midnight, when my partner and I were working a two-man felony car. At least this concept of policing remained: we were fully staffed one night and the overlap shift I worked occasionally had the luxury of fielding a two-man car designated for special problem areas of the city. This was a plain car with no overhead light bar or police markings on the outside of the car. We had a red light inside the car we could place on the rearview mirror in the event of a traffic stop or responding Code 3 (emergency call, with lights and siren) to any situation. We also were liberated from the normal duty of responding to radio calls and allowed to roam. This gave us the freedom to be proactive, to back up any hot call, and to be in a position to prevent crime by using the element of surprise. For cops, these are the fun times and one has to enjoy their job to do it well. We are given the public trust, armed with the constitution and the sacred duty to perform a job that protects our community. I was the book man for this particular evening.

While driving through the south end of our city, we saw a car being driven by two gang members. Yes, we knew they were gang members. They were clearly under the influence (alcohol or drugs) and were driving much like the duster I told you about earlier in this chapter. This wasn't profiling or prejudice, this was based on well-learned experience, the rule of law and training.

My partner and I knew we had good PC (probable cause) to pull them over and investigate. I hung the red spotlight onto the rearview mirror and activated the siren. They drove a few blocks, just outside our city's limits. They definitely wanted to get back to their own gang-infested neighborhood. This is a common tactic for these guys: to return to their turf to gain the advantage of familiar territory and the assistance of their fellow gangsters. After a couple more yelps of the siren, the driver stopped his car right smack dab in the middle of an intersection.

My gut feeling told me we were going to have a fight on our hands. I did what I was trained to do and broadcasted over the police radio that we were "10-7 on a vehicle" and gave the vehicle description and our location. I had barely hung up the mike when the passenger and driver lurched out of the car and looked as if they just woke up out of bed. I noticed the passenger walk away from the car and he strode by me doing the moonwalk. As Yogi Berra once said, "it was like déjà vu all over again."

I walked alongside him for a few feet towards the sidewalk, talking very slowly and calmly to him. I knew what I had and did not want this guy to go ballistic. There is a certain calm that comes with knowing your job, and I knew what had to be done. My partner was dealing with the driver.

While the passenger was completely ignoring my request to stop, I noticed the profuse sweating and could see his heart pounding through his shirt. I did not want a brawl, especially since he was dusted.

I had to think fast: How can I control this guy quickly and get to my partner?

Luckily for me, the intersection was small, and now the moonwalker and I were on the sidewalk, in front of a corner house surrounded by a chain link fence. Not one word I was saying to this guy was being acknowledged. The problem was I could hear my partner now starting to fight with his suspect. I had to improvise fast.

I needed to speed cuff him, but not behind his back as we were taught in the academy. So I instinctively slapped one cuff on him and the other cuff onto the support post of the fence. At least now I didn't have to worry about this guy going off, as my sole purpose now was to get to my partner.

I ran towards my partner, Bob, who was now on the ground, rolling around in the street with the suspect. Anyone who has been in a fight knows the duration seems like a lifetime but is typically only a few minutes. The suspect actually had a slight advantage since he was not wearing a level IIIA vest (which then was like the backseat cushion of a 65 Chevy) and 15 pounds worth of equipment on his body. Not an excuse, just saying. Anyway, I tried to put a wrist lock on the suspect while my partner grabbed the other arm.

This guy just outstretched his arms, broke free and threw me to the curb five feet away. He stood upright and now the three of us were standing and wrestling for a position of control. All the while, my partner and I are telling the suspect to stop resisting and place his hands behind his back and all would be OK. He took me and my partner back to the ground, then again broke free again, and started to walk away.

He only walked a few feet from us and as we re-engaged him, he turned and was now trying to grab our gun belts. Let me make a critical point here: all bets are off when this happens. If the general public should be advised of anything that will escalate a confrontation and get them killed, it's that you NEVER go for a cop's gun. Again, race or politics is not an issue here. It's the behavior that dictates the response.

This is not rocket science, if a combative suspect is trying to pull out an officer's gun from its holster, it means the suspect intends to arm himself and will have the means to use lethal force on the public or the cop. Too many cops have been killed in such confrontations. Let's cut through the bullshit—if someone is psychotic enough in the first place to fight with a cop, let alone go for his gun, they are entertaining a suicide wish. This cannot happen and stopping a threat such as this by any means necessary is allowed and lawful. The public needs to know and accept this. I'll take my chances with a jury rather than die at the hands of an armed criminal high on drugs. There truly is no such thing as a fair fight.

All the Monday morning quarterbacks out there might say, "Why not use your pepper spray?" Well, under PCP, you are in essence, tranquilized, so you feel no pain and you won't feel your tear ducts being irritated by tear gas, so that option is off the table. If we pulled our guns out, we would no doubt give him a better opportunity to grab the firearm and shoot us or force us to shoot him. We were not quite there yet, but it was close.

This was also in the days before Tasers were issued, so we were left with batons, flashlights, chokeholds, and fists. (Saps, or weighted leather impact weapons, were also no longer allowed by a majority of police departments, including ours, at this time). The PR-24 baton is an effective tool, but as Murphy's Law would have it, my partner lost his in the street during the tussle and mine fell out of my baton ring when I jumped out of the car to deal with the passenger. The only thing left were our flashlights, fists, and guns.

I struggled to control the suspect who was now trying to reach for my holster. I was able to put him in the control hold, but I only had one of his arms. My partner delivered a flurry of strikes to him with his flashlight. It must have got his attention since we were starting to finally control him. Also, the neighborhood was now alive with fellow gang members and their respective families out on their porches witnessing the melee.

He let his guard down for a few seconds and we were able to tackle him onto the ground and finally handcuff him. Remember, there were TWO of us dealing with him. If I had been by myself, I would have shot him. Thus, the partner concept works.

By this time, the neighborhood was getting vocal with us and it was getting ugly. Once cuffed, I returned to the police car to radio for help. (My portable radio had also flown off my belt during this encounter.) My arm was nearly broken when the suspect threw me to the curb, but I only had adrenaline in my system, not PCP, so it started to let me know as it sent shockwaves of pain up to my shoulder.

I wish body cameras had been invented back then. This was before the Rodney King incident and if there was a video of our traffic stop from beginning to end, showing every ounce of resistance the suspect unleashed on my partner and I, the King videotape would have looked like a ballet dance compared to how we had to fight that night.

Anyway, during the fight, the suspect sustained a broken collar bone, wrist, and arm. By the time we cleared the scene, the entire neighborhood was out, yelling and letting me and my partner, along with the rest of the backup units on scene, know just how our family lineage evolved, starting with the maternal side. I wish they had known their neighbor who was rushed to a local hospital at their expense and realized the danger he posed to society by driving around under the influence of narcotics and being a gang member in the commission of a crime.

When my partner and I got to the hospital, we interviewed the suspect, who had just given us the mixed martial arts tryout. After he was Mirandized (advised of his constitutional rights per the Miranda rights, otherwise known as the Fifth Amendment), he waived his right to remain silent and told us he had done a speedball AND smoked a sherm before he and his buddy went out for a ride. A speedball is a mixture of cocaine and heroin that is injected directly into the vein. This is the same concoction that killed the famous comedic actor John Belushi and a few other celebrities and common folks. Amazingly during this interview, our suspect actually had the wherewithal to apologize for his actions. Perhaps a glimpse of remorse entered into that cocktail he put into his bloodstream. Nonetheless, the moonwalker and his partner who had been chained to the fence both went to jail.

It became obvious to me after a short while as a patrol officer that those drugs really do screw up people's lives and make them act pretty irresponsibly. I have never seen anyone take a "hit" or "geeze up" (slang for injecting heroin into your veins) then act in such a way that I would want to hang out with him or her. Drugs come with lots of penalties, ranging from failed personal relationships and an inability to gain successful employment, to health and mental issues, criminal behavior, imprisonment, and—the ultimate penalty for the "casual" user—death.

On another night in 1986, again around midnight, I was in a one-man car when the radio silence was shattered with our dispatcher sending out a series of three beeps, then calmly broadcasting what every cop prepares for, "Man with a gun, units responding, you're authorized Code 3."

Dispatch put out the location and designated the appropriate area units to respond. I listened intently to the radio for an update. Minutes later, the next radio broadcast was made by my partners using their portable radios, breathing heavy and requesting help for a "shots fired, man down" situation. I was assigned to our northern most beat and was already rolling toward our downtown area anticipating them needing more assistance.

While en route, dispatch called my unit and said "14 Adam, roll to assist, Code 3." These types of situations tend to be very intense, with lots of confusion thrown in and a lot of people coming out to see what is going on. Traffic is usually a mess and a crime scene perimeter has to be established. Not to mention that bodies may be on the ground, more suspects may be involved, persons with injuries may be running around, and of course the citizens and officers involved must be cared for. When I arrived, I saw a man fighting with paramedics while being placed onto a stretcher and loaded into an ambulance. I thought for a guy who was just shot, he sure had a lot of fight left in him. Without being cynical, my experience told me that it was a safe assumption that the suspect was on drugs.

My sergeant asked me if I could accompany responding officers to the hospital to assist with obtaining statements from any witnesses, family, or the suspect. I did so, and when I got to the hospital, the suspect was still verbally abusive and strapped to the hospital bed. He was yelling profanities at everyone who walked by his room. I was asked to try to interview him and get his statement before he became unconscious. I tried, but he then began moaning and was unable to speak coherently. I next met with some of his family and other witnesses who were at the hospital.

I told them that he had been shot by police and would give them more information as the night progressed. The family was agitated so I said I would return. I walked back through the ER room to meet with my fellow officers and detectives. They had not been physically hurt during the incident. Emotionally hurt is another topic.

While walking through the hallways, a doctor frantically yelled out to me "Hey officer, get in here quick, I need some help." Alright, I thought, and I asked him what I could do for him. He was working on a patient who had just been stabbed and suffered a collapsed lung. The doctor had already made an incision into this guy's left side to insert a breathing tube but was unable to put the tube in due to another life-threatening wound the patient had suffered. The doctor asked me to slip the tube into the side of this guy while he dealt with the other wound. He had already started the procedure and said "just push it in a ways."

Well, with this highly technical advice from a doctor and an apparent urgency to let this guy breathe a little easier, I did as I was told. This man let out a blood curdling moan as I pushed the tube in. While the doctor did his thing, I did mine, and after a few ghoulish minutes, I could hear the air flowing in and out of the tube and then the guy passed out. The doctor finished up with his end of the problem and thanked me.

Let me say one thing about doctors: I have the utmost respect and admiration for all public safety jobs, such as firefighters and especially medical personnel be they paramedics, EMTs, nurses, or doctors. They patch these people up, bring them back from "code blue," perform as first responders to bloody situations, and most of the time keep the suspect alive to face the music. They see the pain, both physical and psychological, that drugs inflict on people. They also help patch up the cops who get hurt fighting this battle.

Getting back to the shooting on this strange night: I needed to get back to the room where the other officers and detectives were gathered. About two hours after we arrived at the hospital, the suspect died of the gunshot wounds. I had the unfortunate duty of advising the family members that were there. As I approached the waiting room, a female asked me how the victim was doing. I always hated this part of the job. No matter what the circumstances are, death by natural causes or due to a violent confrontation, it is one of life's most difficult conversations to have to tell someone that their loved one has died. Their reaction was to be expected. Instant tears from some, then screaming broke out from the other family members who were in the waiting room. They started to throw chairs and it was as if a hurricane was let loose. I figured the last thing they wanted to see was a blue suit and a badge, so I left them to grieve.

This was a tragedy, for both the victim and the officers involved. Then, without fail, the usual lawsuits subsequently erupted as a result of any officer-involved shooting where a death occurs. What I have yet to describe are the events that led up to the shooting.

A few hours before I received the radio dispatch of "Shots fired," the now deceased was home drinking and watching television. According to interviews, he was a casual drug user with previous arrests but nothing heavy, at least until that night. Yes, there is that word again, casual, which is ghostly, like the word "*casualty*."

Witnesses said he was drunk and started to "do some LSD and PCP." After a while, he suddenly became belligerent, grabbed the remote control of his television set and walked out into the evening into a well-traveled intersection. He was yelling at oncoming traffic and raised the remote control with a two-handed stance, as if he was holding a pistol and simulated shooting at the oncoming cars. You can probably see the recipe for disaster on this one. It was dark outside and the local neighbors made the 911 board light up like a Christmas tree with frantic calls of a "Man with a gun, standing in the middle of the street, pointing it at vehicles passing by."

With this information, our units arrived and saw this man holding a gun (the remote) pointing it in all directions. The officers took up tactical positions behind cover and repeatedly ordered him to drop the "gun." They are trained peace officers who themselves use firearms in their jobs. They know what a gun looks like and believed he too was armed with a pistol. The public had called upon their Police Department with 911 calls of a man holding a gun standing in their streets terrorizing cars as they passed by. It was dark outside. It was too dark for them to see that it wasn't really a gun. What if you or your loved ones drove by a man holding a gun and pointing it at your car simulating firing the weapon? How would you feel? How would you react?

Never mind the fact that this man was not really holding a gun, but rather a television remote control device. He held it between his thumb and forefinger with the long end of the remote atop his pointer finger. His bottom fingers were coiled in a two-handed gripping fashion, thereby giving any reasonable person the impression that he was holding a gun.

Yes, one would have to be on drugs to do something so fatally stupid. After the cops ordered him to drop it, begged him to drop it, he pointed the "gun" at them. The officers fired and ultimately killed him. Even while dying in the street, he continued to be physically and verbally combative, fighting with police and paramedics, to the end.

I dare any one to say the cops used excessive force or could have done something else. Defense attorneys would argue that the officers should have negotiated with him, or walked up to him and politely asked him to put the gun down. That is how cops and civilians are killed. Then the same defense attorneys would argue the cops were scared to act and used improper tactics if the suspect actually fired into passing vehicles. Damned if you do, damned if you don't. This is the bullshit and reality of our job.

Incidentally, when the lawsuit went to court, typical public reaction was to be expected. "How dare those racist cops use excessive force and kill an innocent man with a remote control?" Thankfully a key witness, not a cop but just an ordinary resident of that neighborhood, testified on behalf of the police. This witness was a retired elderly citizen who happened to be a former Marine Corps firearms instructor, was combat experienced, and knew handguns. He saw the deranged man in the street that night and testified that the man appeared to be holding a semi-automatic pistol.

That was based on his years of military experience. The suspect clearly fooled everyone, including the local neighbors who made the 911 calls, eye witnesses of the event, and the police officers who responded. The officers were correctly found not guilty of violating anybody's civil rights, but they still carry the scars of a tragedy, knowing that a human life was needlessly sacrificed all because of a "casual" drug episode.

During my time as a patrol officer, I started to become jaded towards the casual drug user. Do you wonder why? It seemed pretty obvious to me that drugs were destroying the very fabric of our society. My next thought was to try to get to the root of the problem, get more proactive rather than reactive. I had heard about the State Narcotics Bureau of CA DOJ, called BNE, and applied for the position of Special Agent.

2

Canary in a Coal Mine

*"Diamonds are nothing more than chunks of coal
that stuck to their jobs"*

— Malcolm Forbes

In the 1880s, mining was a way life for much of the United States. Without the benefit of technology and science, crude methods were used to detect poisonous gasses associated with mining for coal and other precious minerals. In a time before animal rights activists, humans used animals to help industrial America move forward. Whether it was teams of horses pulling heavy metal plows for days on end or cattle herded across states lines, we needed animals to survive. Thus the canary. It was sensitive to certain natural gases and could detect its presence before its human partners. Unfortunately, the bird would die in the process, but a human life was saved before going into the bowels of a cave where toxic gasses awaited. Have you seen the 1977 movie *Close Encounters of the Third Kind*? Remember the mountain scene and the military troops? The bird lay dead at the bottom of the cage after it detected the gasses in the area where humans would be walking around. Much like that sentinel bird, so were the State Narcs and other first responders who courageously went into those clandestine drug labs to save a neighborhood. Let's not forget all the 9/11 first responders who contracted cancers and suffer other permanent physical injuries due to the toxin exposures. Some even died. All these responders went into a hazardous chemical waste environment (the twin towers wreckage site) to clean it up and recover our fellow human beings.

While I was processing for the position of Special Agent with the California Department of Justice, the narcotic epidemic was in full swing. After another round of testing and selection and a new background process, I made the cut. I was offered a job in the fall of 1987 and left the police department only to jump into my next police academy, this one with the California Department of Justice. This group of cops was different than my first time with a class of police recruits. Then, the majority of us were very young, fresh out of college, in our early twenties and not too experienced.

This academy class was noticeably different from my first police academy class. The entire Special Agent class, which graduated 23 of us, were all former cops from various agencies with the exception of one trainee (Joel who was one of those individuals with that sense of humor sorely needed in a job like this). This was a seasoned group of recruits and we were all taking the logical next step in the law enforcement evolution; that is, to become full-time, plain clothes investigators assigned to work major narcotics. This Special Agent academy lasted only seven weeks, thank goodness.

We were treated more like professionals than entry-level boot camp recruits. The academic curriculum focused on the Health and Safety Code and other specialty missions related to conducting high-level investigations initiated by the California Attorney General's Office.

We also became quasi-chemists since we had to know not only the laws regarding narcotic enforcement, but also the types of drugs that were out there and how they were grown, synthesized, or manufactured. We became expert in these types of unique investigations, bringing to bear all the tools of the trade, such as specialized surveillance equipment, the latest investigative techniques, and methods of operations used by the major narcotic traffickers. The State of California and the country were experiencing a huge drug problem and, unfortunately, so were the police agencies tasked to stop this crime.

Sadly, just as the general public was tormented by drugs, law enforcement was also susceptible to their temptations. In my Special Agent class, one of my classmates who was a narcotic detective prior to accepting the Special Agent job was fired during our academy. He decided to socialize with a drug user and was in possession of a vial of cocaine labeled with an evidence sticker from his old police department. He had crossed the line but the system worked, ferreted him out, and punished him. We have no room for this type of crooked cop. This hit close to home since we were all classmates but it didn't surprise some of the more veteran cops. They too each had horror stories of fellow cops who checked out of their role as peace officers. Again, cops are a reflection of the population they police and both the good and sometimes the bad infiltrate our ranks.

I graduated this academy and went to work at a Southern California field office. My first day on the job resulted in being part of an entry team and actually *serving* a narcotic search warrant instead of being the one to wait on the front porch. I will admit, being a uniformed officer, wearing a badge on my chest, a hat, a baton, and a radio blaring from my person gave the public a clear impression that I was a police officer. Now working as a plain-clothes officer and wearing jeans, T-shirt, and a blue windbreaker with a few patches saying "POLICE," left me somewhat subdued. Nevertheless, when I arrived at the office at 0800 hours, I received the keys to my state car and a briefing sheet detailing the search warrant operation. I had already been issued my safety gear but back then we were still pretty Spartan when "suiting up" for search warrant operations.

No helmets, machine guns, flash bangs, or ballistic shields. We were issued a Colt .45 caliber pistol, a DOJ baseball cap, police windbreaker, a bulletproof vest, and a set of handcuffs. If we wanted anything more in the way of firepower, 12-gauge shotguns were kept at each field office under lock and key. They had to be checked out for any operation, then returned immediately at the end of the event. If you were in the field and needed it, someone had to go back to the office and get it. Times have changed; but at least then, this was all that was truly necessary.

After our briefing, we rolled out to a suspected methamphet-amine dealer's house that lived in the Orange County area. I was assigned as the "number three man" in the stack. The stack is the line-up order when assembling at the front door of a structure.

True to form, we met up with the local police units and they accompanied us to the front door of the house. In our briefing, we were told that prior surveillance and reconnaissance missions indicated that this dope dealer was your typical "tweeker," meaning that he was a meth user, ultra- paranoid, slept in the daytime, and was up all night and into the morning.

He differed from the typical tweeker in one way. This guy was usually manufacturing methamphetamine and he was so high from making the drug, he couldn't go sleep if he wanted to. Because of his "amped up" (hyper) mental state and his delusional fear of being watched by big brother, he installed video cameras on the outside perimeter of his house. This way he could see anyone coming up to the residence. The problem with this, or you might want to call it a blessing, was that our tweeker also suffered from another side effect from doing meth: the inability to sit still. He couldn't sit in front of a surveillance monitor to guard his house if his life depended on it.

As we knocked on the front door, we announced in a loud voice several times "Police, search warrant, demand entry, we have a search warrant." When no one answered the door, we used our battering ram and punched the door in. We entered the house and conducted our room clearing tactics until we found the suspect, placed him in custody, and put out a Code 4. As we conducted our search, we found evidence of clandestine laboratory glassware, tubing, and residue of freshly cooked methamphetamine in the garage. This was the first of many speed labs I would encounter during my BNE career.

The "speed cooker" (meth manufacturer) is a sick human being. If the general public only knew exactly what goes into manufacturing methamphetamine! The same chemicals that are found in gasoline, pool cleaning solvents, fireworks, nerve gas, and a host of other toxic products make up this truly dangerous drug. As a matter of fact, one of the main chemicals used in the manufacturing process is a known teratogen. For the non-chemist, this is defined by the Embryo Project Encyclopedia as an extremely poisonous compound that can alter human DNA if just mere milligrams are ingested. In English, if you put this in your system and you decide one day to have kids, there is a high chance of the children being hideously deformed. The definition of teratogen translates from the Greek word, "monster." You get the picture.

During the early years of my BNE career, I saw meth labs that not only ruined the lives of the cooker and user, but also the lives of innocent kids. We discovered one particular lab site in the beautiful and scenic high desert community of the Antelope Valley, just outside of Los Angeles. We developed probable cause and obtained a search warrant to further our investigation of methamphetamine manufacturing at this site. We knocked and announced as usual and waited. When we received no response, we forced entry into the residence.

My partners were pretty good with a battering ram, so the door was quickly and efficiently taken off its hinges, and we were in. Once inside, I saw two kids, about 2 and 4 years old, lying on the floor watching television. The mother was in a bedroom, and the father (our suspect) was also lounging in the bedroom, in a trance. The adults were arrested without incident and the kids were saved, but that was the only positive aspect about this raid.

On closer inspection and subsequent search of the property, chemicals, glassware, equipment and some finished product (methamphetamine) were found—more than enough to illustrate to a jury that this man was involved in the manufacture and distribution of meth. However, the inside of the home was not your typical house. The walls of the living room and bedroom were adorned with family photos. The odd thing was that the photos depicted the lady of the house (the suspect's wife and children's mother) in various extremely graphic sexual acts with her hubby and about 20 of his closest friends and girlfriends. Okay, pornography is legal, this is America, we have the First Amendment, and it was their home; but do you really want your toddlers seeing this? Also the house was in squalor. I found several half-eaten sandwiches on the living room floor, the bread hardened like rock, and cockroaches crawling over them. There were ants climbing the corners of each wall and rat droppings throughout the house. The kids were in pull-ups, coughing, and malnourished, and they looked like the kids in a third-world country dying of hunger. The smell of urine and human feces cloaked the interior of the house.

Furniture, appliances, carpeting, and flooring were torn and tattered except for the television and stereo. They were immaculate. State-of-the-art, hi-fi electronic components and television, accompanied by a vast array of videotapes. Since some of these crooks are known to record themselves in the commission of their crimes, including drive-by shootings and assaults, as well as making meth, we had the legal right to view the tapes in search of additional evidence. Unfortunately, the videos only depicted the lady of the house with the same cast of characters on display in the photographs on the walls. Later we learned there was an exchange of sexual favors for drugs and the furtherance of their narcotic enterprise. Not a big surprise, huh? This was not an inner city, but a rural, desert community and white suspects. I have seen crime affect all walks of life, regardless of race.

Outside of the house, their business spilled over to the landscape. The rear and side yards were used for dumping the chemical by-products that are generated from a meth cook. This muck of misery completely destroyed every living plant within 100 feet of the house, and when the county health department responded, they immediately cordoned off the area and told us they would declare this property a contaminated site and request complete demolition of the existing structure and bulldozing of the soil to a depth and circumference that would render it safe until further testing could be done. How would you like to be the realtor trying to sell that house or land?

The children were handed over to Child Protective Services so they could receive basic care such as food, clean clothes, and guardians that were not high on drugs. Back then, arrests and seizures like these led to a brief decline in the methamphetamine problem for that area, but as with all such victories, it was fleeting. Up to the mid-2000s, California was considered a "source" state as the nation's leading producer of methamphetamine.

This has since changed due to tougher U.S. laws on the precursors and other chemicals needed to manufacture meth. Mexico now has the distinction of being the largest producer of methamphetamine, but California crooks continue to try and manufacture their own. The manufacturing will never be eradicated, but it has been slowed.

I have seen this drug up close both in its raw and finished stages. I have been in numerous clan labs (short for clandestine labs) and have witnessed the deadly consequences of its manufacture. In one graphic instance, I responded to a residence where one such lab blew up. The wannabe chemist did not follow a simple yet important rule during the process and a chain reaction occurred, resulting in a violent explosion. The neighbors in this upscale neighborhood in Southern California were rocked by the explosion. Then a half-naked man, rendered blind and with burns all over his body, was running up and down the block screaming. His clothes (what was left of them) were saturated with the stench and stains from the chemicals he used during this "cook" in the basement of his mother's house.

The local fire and police personnel had arrived prior to my BNE partners and I. Together, we inspected the site of the lab, which happened to be a basement beneath this very nice home. The firemen had extinguished the flames and we were able to see the aftermath of the explosion. I donned my "bunny suit" (a white protective suit like a chemist working for the CDC wears) and mask, and I took a look around. Red stains were splattered on the walls and ceiling of the room. Laboratory glassware containing a red, thick sludge was on a heating source with most of its contents now acting as wallpaper for the room. Cans of Freon, red phosphorous, rubber tubing, glass beakers, plastic funnels, and other chemicals associated with the manufacturing process were inside the room. The smell was nauseating, and that was through a mask. (Remember that PCP traffic stop I described earlier? This smell made that one seem like a rose garden.)

The reason for his death one week later was him committing suicide after being released on bail. He was exposed to this chemical cook, and no doubt the years of drug use prior to that were a contributing factor. A person can get high from smelling the fumes while the drug is being made. Remember, these dope cookers are not NASA scientists and tend to cook like probably most of our moms did. (Sorry, Mom; no offense intended.) That is to say, they have recipes for the manufacturing process, but they tend to ad lib it. A pinch here, a drop there, and they make it haphazardly. They also become lax and think of this as a batch of brownies. As this happens, that is when the accidents occur. The coup de grâce for this suspect was the inherent danger in clandestinely making meth. Sure, if he had access to a university's science lab with all the sterile, safety equipment and permission from the dean, he possibly could have avoided some of the dangers; but he did not.

I forgot to mention that during a methamphetamine cook, a dangerous gas called phosphine is created. It is a wonder that anyone survives these clan lab cooks.

What a way to go. Perhaps his family and friends knew of his "hobby" and neglected to tell the police, a friend, or some other agency that could have helped him. How many others did he poison with his product? You don't have to be a genius to make this garbage; I guess that is why they call it dope.

Back to the gas. A quick history lesson for those of you who do not know about chemical warfare: Phosphine gas was first developed by the Germans during World War I. This gas was used during trench warfare and used on enemy troops. It is classified as a nerve agent made to damage the central nervous system by causing nausea, loss of motor skills and cerebral functions, shutting down the liver and kidneys, and ultimately resulting in death.

This gas was so cruel in its effects that the Chemical Weapons Conference outlawed its use during warfare. It has not been used since the end of WWII. A side note: in the early 1990s this gas was resurrected and was used by a psychopathic dictator on his own people. His name was Saddam Hussein.

Do we want our society to legalize this? These chemicals in and of themselves are toxic, why would one mix and "cook" them to create something that was deemed heinous enough to be outlawed by the rules of war? Neighborhoods are put at risk whenever one of these crooks decides to play mad scientist. I ask these people when I arrest them why they do it. Unequivocally the answer is "for the high and the money, man."

If someone wants to use a drug like this, I submit (sarcastically) that maybe they should take a gallon of simple, premium grade, high octane automobile fuel and drink shots of it during the course of an evening. This is already a legal substance, government controlled and sold publicly. The government does a few things right and gasoline production is one of them. This will give them the same taste and benefit of methamphetamine so they can poison their DNA for their kids to remember them by, but without endangering the neighbors.

Methamphetamine as a raw product is essentially chemical sewage that will keep you up for days on end. If done right, the finished product is usually a clean-looking white powder. I mentioned the fly-by-the-seat-of-your-pants cook, and sometimes the end result is a yellow or "peanut butter" meth, as it is affectionately referred to by the users. It has the same effect as the white powder but did not get processed cleanly so it appears dirty. This drug is always manufactured clandestinely and because of this, the facilities used to make this stuff are usually lacking in the Occupational

Safety and Health Administration (OSHA) certifications needed for housing this type of toxin. Another quick history lesson: German troops in the First World War wanted to keep its soldiers awake on the battlefield and give them an edge over their enemy. That was why the amphetamines were initially developed. They were later perverted and used by another dictator during a time of war—Adolf Hitler.

In the late 1990s, I was assisting one of our clan lab teams with the service of a search warrant where a lab was suspected. Now I have participated in thousands of briefings held by a host of law enforcement agencies and bar none, the DOJ put on a very thorough and professional briefing that includes the reason we are taking the enforcement action, a brief history of the investigation, personnel assignments, and contingency plans for the worst case scenario, and then we open it up for any questions. By doing this, everyone is crystal clear on what has to be done and how we are going to do it.

Back in the day, it was commonplace to just say something like, "You cover the front door, I'll go to the back and you four go inside and clear it." That was 30 years ago. Now it's a lot more in depth. Good planning for such raids is vital to protect both the public and the cops.

Returning to that search warrant I was telling you about: we briefed and hit the door of the residence located in a typical middle-class neighborhood in the city of El Monte. At the briefing, it was discussed and anticipated that this could be a lab site. Knowing this, we understood the risks, whether it was an armed suspect with an AK-47 waiting inside or the invisible enemy, a toxic cloud that could kill us in a few seconds. The brutal and unforgiving part about this type of police work is that we take the risk of being exposed to an array of chemical waste manufactured by the suspect. BNE Special Agents are highly trained and act as both hazardous waste experts and a SWAT team when entering into these situations; but we can only plan for so many contingencies. This is another reason why it's called a safety retirement.

All the best training and gear cannot prevent the unknown and only offers some modicum of protection. In this case, we served the warrant for suspected drug sales at the house, but we had no hard evidence that there was a lab at the site as well. So we donned our usual raid gear, without respirator equipment. As we went to the front door, it was barred up pretty good so we opted for entry through a side door toward the rear yard. After complying with the legal knock/notice requirement and receiving no response, we knocked down the back door with our battering ram. The team entered and conducted room clearing tactics. Within a few seconds, I felt as if I had swallowed a glass of rock salt. My throat was burning, along with everyone else's. We actually held our breath, completed an accelerated search of the premises and found no one inside, but did see a clandestine laboratory set up in the back room. We got the hell out after a quick clearing of the structure. The other part of the group, led by our clan lab team experts, then went in, all suited up like Apollo 13 astronauts.

Based on our description, the clean-up team located and dismantled the lab. Paramedics were called for my group and when they arrived on scene, they told us that our throats were sore due to experiencing "Red P" burn. Apparently the residue was still in the air of the house and this chemical is one that was used during this particular manufacturing process. "Red P" is actually slang for the chemical "red phosphorous", which is used primarily in the pyrotechnic industry for fireworks. I was told to suck on peppermints and that would alleviate the stinging sensation from the Red P. I thought to myself, this is bullshit, but it was part of the job.

I did as they suggested and survived it and the burning sensation disappeared after a few hours, but who really knows what this garbage does to our systems, especially after numerous exposures to it? Worse yet are the "cookers," who knowingly expose their innocent family or neighbors to this toxic waste. I knew this was not a specialty I would want to do for any length of time. I take my hat off to those law enforcement professionals who do that task day in and day out, performing the job of a nuclear hazardous waste specialist and a cop. I also pray that no more innocent kids like the ones I found at these lab sites grow up to be like their parents and that they get the help they need. As for those parents who would abdicate their roles so they could make a buck on this poison and want to legalize it, I truly believe the saying "what comes around, goes around."

3

The Coca Plant

"Cocaine is God's way of saying you make too much money"

— ROBIN WILLIAMS

Cocaine is the party drug. Before discos and Studio 54 in New York, before comedians like Robin Williams and Richard Pryor made jokes about getting high, and before professional athletes like NBA player Roy Tarpley had a brilliant career cut short due to cocaine addiction, cocaine was used by society's elite. For centuries the natives in South American villages used it to stay awake and work long hours doing physical labor. The laborer would chew on the leaf of the coca plant to get a quick surge of energy needed to do the farming of various crops, including coffee and the coca plant.

There is archaeological evidence in Ecuador regarding the use of this drug as early as 3000 BC. It was considered the divine plant of the Incas and was controlled by that tribe through the 16[iii] century. When the Incas were conquered by the Spanish, mining became a business for this country. The Indian laborers began chewing the leaves of the coca plant to give them energy for the long work day. Each person would chew two ounces of leaves a day, which is equivalent to about half a gram of cocaine. This plant only grows in specific areas of South America and when the drug cartels realized they could exploit a naturally occurring substance found in the jungles of nature to be the single most desired drug in the world, they became overnight billionaires.

Cocaine found a huge market in the free world, especially in the good ol' USA. It was actually used medicinally as a cure for alcohol and morphine addiction. In the early 1900s cocaine was used in small amounts in some beverages, like Coca-Cola, but was ultimately removed as one of the ingredients. It is used today in legitimate medical procedures such as a topical anesthetic to numb surfaces like the mouth and nose, along with other medical uses. Pharmaceutical-grade cocaine is typically found in liquid form called cocaine hydrochloride.

Cocaine became well known at gatherings of society's rich and famous, such as at Hollywood parties or New York night clubs. Depending on where you lived in the 1970s and continuing through the 1980s, it was very prevalent. However, it was mostly found in the big cities and its price actually went up in value, an indication that law enforcement was making a difference. But since the 1990s, the demand for this drug has been constant and a matter of simple economics. Just like the stock market, prices go up and down, but the U.S. customers crave it. Therefore competition is alive and well. Supply and demand theory works. The crack epidemic is another story.

When I was a young police officer in the 1980s, cocaine was making a huge splash on the social scene. I remember responding to numerous disturbance calls at residences and local bars where people were under the influence of cocaine and simply gave up being "responsible" adults trying to have a good time. They became belligerent, hostile jerks. This was true to form since cocaine is a stimulant; it gave people a sense of bravado that they normally wouldn't have. It is bad enough breaking up fights involving drunks. At least in those fights, the drunks are slow to react, their senses are similar to being anaesthetized, and you can always get the upper hand. When cocaine is involved, the fights are more intense and the assaults are more violent due to the combatant's stimulated condition, hyper sense of alertness and reflexes, and subjective feelings of invincibility.

There are a few facts about cocaine that you should understand before I share my stories. First, a "line" of coke is about .25 milligrams. The high can last up to five hours but when you crash, you need at least the same amount or more of the drug to achieve the same high.

This is the hook for most drugs. The human body develops a tolerance for drugs and alcohol and the more you do, the harder you fall, then the more of the drug you need to do just to get back to that initial high.

I will relate this to alcohol consumption. Those of you that are teetotalers may have difficulty with this one, but here goes: Remember your first beer? Odds are you don't since it probably got you drunk very quickly. Now fast forward your body about 10 years. Provided you are now a "casual" drinker and have been so for years, a single beer might as well be a glass of water.

Your body naturally develops a tolerance for the alcohol level you put into your system and more than likely (unless you weigh 90 pounds) it takes a couple of beers to get that same euphoria you felt when you had your first one. Without going into a dissertation on human biology and alcoholism, you can see how once a person becomes addicted, he or she needs to drink a lot to get to the point where an alcoholic feels the "buzz." And an addiction to drugs works the same way.

A physical dependence occurs that can be managed, but never cured. Programs such as Alcoholics Anonymous and others provide tried and tested methods that help most alcoholics handle the habit. However, the psychological addiction also kicks in. The same is true for tobacco use. One or two cigarettes will get you the nicotine high, but the hard-core smoker needs several packs a day to get that result since their body has developed a tolerance and the physical addiction to nicotine is voracious. They also have the psychological aspect that is equally addictive if not more so.

And consider marijuana cigarettes. These will make the big tobacco use of the 20th century look like child's play. This social experiment will haunt our country for decades to come and is already going to cost us a generation. I'll discuss this more in upcoming chapters.

Back to cocaine: It is especially cruel because it not only develops the physical dependence, it also attacks a part of the brain that acutely remembers the euphoric feeling it got and now you have a vehement psychological dependence. Both these factors make it an extremely hard substance to kick.

Cocaine is expensive and ***illegal.*** I saw through my experiences in law enforcement that those who are addicted to coke (cocaine) versus their alcoholic counterparts are a more violent and mentally ill group. In all my years as a cop, I have never seen a drunk kill another drunk for a beer. Nor have I seen a drug cartel, organized crime group, or terrorist network order the assassinations of rivals over a shot of tequila. With narcotics like cocaine, heroin, and marijuana, it happens all too often.

The frequency of cocaine-related deaths, murders, suicides, assaults, kidnappings, rapes, robberies, and burglaries (generally committed to support and traffic this hard-core drug) is exponentially greater than the same crimes committed by alcoholics. I personally saw the effect of these crimes perpetrated on our communities in the Golden State, not from the alcoholic, but from the drug user and trafficker. Cocaine proved to be even more addicting and has turned upside down inner cities and destroyed families across this country.

As a patrol officer I responded to a disturbance call one evening at a local bar where a patron (the suspect), according to witnesses, did a "line or two of coke" then got into an altercation with another patron. I arrived on scene and paramedics were already taking the victim to the hospital, where he died later that morning. Here is what I figured out had happened: The suspect started a fight with this other patron after he had done some coke. He started a fist fight with the poor guy and then picked up a thick, heavy glass beer mug and smashed it against the victim's head, ultimately killing him. All the way to jail the suspect kept saying, "I didn't mean to hit him, he'll probably be OK, right officer?" Little did he know that when I booked him at our jail for assault with a deadly weapon, the charge would become murder a few hours later.

A single moment in time when poor judgment was utilized by this man cost him a lengthy prison sentence, destroyed his family and friendships, and more importantly, took another human life. All needlessly; all for a cocaine high.

After I became a State Narcotic Agent, I was assigned to a Special Operations Unit (SOU). One of my first cases involved a cocaine distribution ring operating in Southern California. I was successful in infiltrating this group with the assistance of another undercover agent from a different law enforcement agency.

Acting in an undercover capacity, I negotiated with a member of the distribution ring, who I will call Maria. Before the meet took place, an extensive briefing was conducted with all contingencies planned for, especially the very real possibility that this may be a "rip off." This refers to the possibility that the suspects may rob the undercover agent instead of completing the sale. Unfortunately, I have lost some of my peers to this exact situation. One must always plan for the worst-case scenario.

The meeting was set and I met with Maria in a public area to talk about purchasing several kilograms of cocaine. I was acting as a wholesale distributor for the drug. A common method of operation for these characters is to buy in bulk, and then dilute the product with a cutting agent such as mannitol to turn a kilogram of coke (1,000 grams) into 2,000 grams. (Kind of sounds like the four patrol cars turning into eight, huh?) Let's do the math: say you buy the kilo for $13,000. Take the 1,000 grams, "step" on it (dilute it) and make it into 2,000 grams. You then sell the 2,000 grams for $100 bucks per gram, and you make *$200,000.* What a country. This is how the trafficker is able to make millions of dollars and why this drug has overtaken coffee as South America's number one export.

During the meeting, I watched her associates check me out and walk around the area, acting as lookouts for their boss. This type of counter surveillance is common for these groups and it assures their boss that the prospective buyer (me) is legitimate. We happen to be better than them, and my cover team was perfectly blended into the surrounding area and was undetectable. It still amazes me to this day that the streets of America are the business grounds for such a deadly product. My officer safety senses were heightened and as I looked for reassurance (back up) during this deal, I was able to pick out a couple of my partners covering me during this tightrope walk that BNE Special Agents can relate to. This gave me peace of mind as I was negotiating for the purchase of several kilograms of cocaine. Maria was satisfied I was for real and said we could do business anytime. I told her to call me when she was ready to sell. She agreed and I left the meeting, along with my cover team to work on another case. Much like hunting, we had to keep moving to find the next target.

Within the next couple of weeks, Maria called and said she was ready to sell one kilo of coke. I put on my undercover role and asked about the other kilos we had discussed. She said she only had one kilo available at this time. I shared my disappointment with her on the lack of merchandise availability but I agreed to buy the one kilo. We had to arrange a location for the sale and she settled on the transaction occurring on a street. I agreed to it and once the cover team was assembled and briefed, we drove to her neighborhood, which was a nice, middle-income residential area. As I drove up in front of a house, she and her cohort were waiting for me.

Her partner-in-crime handed me the kilogram of coke, which was concealed in a shoe box. Yes, it was a tennis shoe box just like the one from my PCP traffic stop years ago when I was a young patrolman. I looked at the kilo in the box and flashed back to that incident from a cold Los Angeles evening a decade ago. Seconds later, I told her it looked good to me and that it would do.

I gave the prearranged signal and my team moved in to make the arrest. All the crooks were caught and the cocaine seized. All suspects were subsequently tried and ultimately convicted. This was a successful operation.

The types of investigations that narcotic enforcement exposes the investigator to is quite varied and at times very intense. One day you and your team are conducting surveillance, following an affluent suspect as he drops off his kids at private school then goes to his yacht in the marina, or you might be in the ghetto of some inner city with drive-by shootings occurring around you.

Narcotic trafficking is a huge money-making venture and people from all walks of life participate in this illegal trade. Intelligence gathering, both on a local and an international basis, is key to knowing the public we serve and our adversaries that wish to do us harm. Surveillance and technology tools are of great assistance, but nothing beats the real-time, on-the-ground contacts with the communities in which we interact and serve. Talking to people, working with the community and knowing what is happening around you is good situational awareness.

With the war against terrorism, a hue and cry was raised, asking, "Why weren't we warned about the 9/11 attacks in New York?" All the satellites and telescopes were not enough to warn our country about a specific threat or attack. Many of the same criticisms took place then as you hear today with our police. Our government and national law enforcement agencies were unfairly accused about the lack of information provided in a timely manner that could have averted this disaster. Yes, we talk about connecting the dots; but it was not their fault as we relied on technology and the goodwill of others to keep such evil deeds from happening to our country. By not allowing a PROACTIVE and LAWFUL approach to the issue, we will always miss out on protecting our communities and our country. This is true for policing as well. Only real-time, on-the-ground, human intelligence can allow us to learn about, prevent, and prepare for an attack—be it from an airplane, a biological weapon, gangs, crime, or tons of cocaine being distributed on our nation's streets.

Our laws should protect the rights of everyone, and the national debate over this will constantly occur. But the debate and the laws should have in mind the protection of all, not just a few.

This problem faces California's Department of Justice as well as local police departments. In the late 1990s and continuing to present day, patrol officers curb proactive efforts in policing. A public contact that is not a call for police service, like conducting a self-initiated stop on an individual who is loitering in front of an

ATM machine or a grammar school, or a traffic stop on a suspicious driver cruising through a neighborhood, is not as easily done for various reasons. A personnel complaint may arise from the encounter; there exists in society and the media a hypersensitivity to law enforcement being on the lookout for unusual activity; and a barrage of lawsuits and complaints hinder a good cop's ability to be proactive.

Also some management philosophies, new laws and legal interpretations of the law deter law enforcement from taking the initiative. This is both a reality and sign of our times. Permissions must be granted to launch certain types of investigations, and new missions, like parole oversight and local jails now housing state prisoners, minimize the time an agency has to be proactive. Law enforcement has been forced to go to the "prevent defense." But as any football fan knows, the only thing the prevent defense does is prevent the team from winning.

Another case I worked in the mid-1990s was as an undercover agent attempting to purchase multiple kilograms of cocaine from a group in the Los Angeles area. This guy, who I'll call "Paul", was setting up a lucrative operation and I was fortunate enough to get next to him and talk about my (supposed) cocaine trafficking activities. He liked what I had to say and after a couple of meetings, a "buy-bust" was set. This is where the undercover agents buy drugs and then immediately arrest the suspects on sight.

The customary briefing took place and my team knew exactly how the deal was to occur. This is another part of police work, especially in narcotic enforcement, when you literally put your life in the hands of your partners. A critical factor in any undercover operation is supervision. My Special Agent Supervisor, Joe, was himself a seasoned undercover operator and a skilled tactician. Without quality leadership from experts in the field, no job can get done. Joe was both our boss and our leader. He made sure we all came home safe. My teammates focused their entire being on me when it was my turn to be the "UC," (undercover agent). Any sign of trouble, including the help or bust signal, was relayed by the special agent who was watching the UC. Those teammates also acted as the cavalry when the time came to move in and make the arrest. Thank you to Victor, Cris, Frank, Andre, and the rest of LA-71.

As I drove up to the house on that particular night, I waved to Paul, who was waiting in front of the carport where we had agreed the deal would take place. With my cover team in place, I went in and shook hands with Paul to start the transaction. I could only see a parked car in the carport and since I was coming in from broad daylight to a dimly lit environment, my eyes had to momentarily adjust to the new lighting. Usually there is a banter that takes place when one is about to buy dope, but in this instance he told me he had it and wanted to show it to me. I looked around and noticed another man in the shadows, standing in the deep left corner of the carport, watching me. Another man then came out from the opposite side and said he would show it (the cocaine) to me.

These are the nuances that told me they had the cocaine and were guarding it. I had no money and they knew that, so the "rip" or "kidnap" scenario was not likely. As I talked to the next suspect, "Joey," he was extremely calm and told me to peek into a duffel bag that was inside the vehicle. I saw he was wearing a T-shirt and something else that made me think these guys were serious about this business. Through Joey's shirt, I saw the imprint of a semi-automatic pistol pressed against his belly. Since this was the weapon I carried, I knew it well. Timing is everything, and being calm is paramount. In an effort to buy myself some time, I asked Joey to open the door of the car so I could see my merchandise.

He did so and I became acutely aware of his pistol and for a second thought about pulling my gun. I knew there were two other guys in addition to him and I was absolutely sure that they too were packing. This was an instance where discretion was the better part of valor. I did not pull my gun. I did what any self-respecting buyer would do: I inspected the cocaine. I leaned into the car, unzipped the bag, and counted a couple of the kilos, each wrapped in yellow tape in the customary rectangular shape. I calmly stood straight up and reacquired the three potential shoot targets.

I looked at Paul and told him everything looked great. He appeared elated and I told him I would be returning within a few minutes so we could finish the transaction. He agreed, while Joey kept his hands at his side staring at me the whole time. The other guy slithered back into the darkened corner of the carport. I thought to myself, this is a hell of a way to earn that safety retirement and gladly walked out of the immediate vicinity. As I was walking back to my car, I gave the bust signal.

This is a moment when the perception of time slows down. I remember walking to my UC car (undercover car) and looking over my shoulder to see him and the others waiting for me to return. He eyeballed the street up and down and watched me as I opened my car door. My job was to buy some time for the team so they could close in. I started up my car to get Paul's attention focused on me, and it worked. Then the cover team appeared from their camouflaged positions and converged on the residence smoothly, like mercury flowing from a broken thermometer. These professionals I worked with were past the phase of screeching their tires and rolling up with lights and sirens. This critical phase, when units move in, could make or break an arrest scene. Too loud, and the crooks hear and see you coming in. They will run, fight, or arm themselves.

A calmer, deliberate approach allowed us to catch them all. My "3" (Joe, the Special Agent Supervisor) called this "swooping," and we did this well. The suspects barely reacted to the team. A short foot pursuit to the backyard and they were all arrested without incident, without a shot being fired. And yes, all the suspects were armed with handguns. We had the upper hand, the preparation and discipline, to execute this operation with precision. No innocent bystanders, cops, or crooks were hurt. The suspects later were found guilty and sentenced to state prison.

Cocaine traffickers are a savvy bunch of individuals. They are always part of a larger network or organization and this makes them challenging to investigate. As I continued my time with BNE in the '90s, large seizures of cocaine were starting to become common. 100, 200, 500 kilos and more were routinely being seized by not only our agency, but the local police, the DEA, and the FBI as well. We were a patient group of Special Agents and as State Narcotic Agents, we had the jurisdiction and capability to go beyond the typical city or county boundaries.

Our patience in one investigation paid off with interest when we seized almost one ton of cocaine. These suspects were good and it required a partnership effort by BNE with local agencies. During this case, I remember being in our cars, hunkered down in a nearby neighborhood, waiting for the identified cocaine smugglers to make their move. It was late at night, cold, and pouring down rain. We had been up for days and were operating on adrenalin (and a healthy dose of fast food and coffee). I remember looking at my partners scattered around me, all catching a combat nap. I had just wrapped myself in my state-issued blanket and was dozing off when the radio crackled. The point man called out activity and sure enough, the crooks were on the move again.

Like the Indy 500, engines started up and off we went into the early morning. Several hours later, we landed at a house in a southern California neighborhood and, with search warrant in hand, we hit the jackpot. Talk about doing the math. Go back to the figure mentioned earlier, except instead of just one kilogram being diluted into multi-grams, this was several hundred kilograms waiting to be diluted and distributed. All were arrested and prosecuted.

That was a *lot* of dollars in potential profits that this organization lost. Granted, a street value of these types of seizures were in the millions of dollars; but it was not the *value* of the dope that was significant, but rather the dope itself and key arrests of their trusted traffickers. The suspects were stopped dead in their tracks and this disrupted their organization. Without a doubt, local dealers suffered a blow (no pun intended) and at least momentarily the drug flow was interrupted.

Cases like this one were fairly routine for years, until resources such as money and manpower ran thin. In addition, the crooks were becoming schooled in the prison and court system on how

American law enforcement operates. Make no mistake about it: prison is a chance for these traffickers to network with each other and some have gotten to the point that they coordinate their criminal enterprises from their prison cells.

A cyclical trend occurred during the '80s, '90s, and early 2000s. The price of cocaine rose and then fell, just like the stock market. When the efforts of law enforcement are working, prices rise and fall, but the demand for the product drives the market. The rule of basic economics still applies. California was, and still is, a hotbed for narcotic traffickers.

This is a fair test of narcotic enforcement efforts, at least within the State of California. Of course cocaine is still on the streets and has not been purged from our society because there exists a supply and demand that is insatiable. Through education and communities investing their guidance of each other, along with an *ongoing and constant* effort by law enforcement, community leaders and government to curb this abuse, we as a society can keep it in check. In the decades I have been involved in this business, the attempts still occur at our borders to smuggle drugs into our country. The high seas are also a route for large amounts of contraband to traverse. Thus, law enforcement efforts will continue to be tested daily at our nation's borders and ports.

This may not sound like a huge and complete eradication of this drug. As mentioned before, I can honestly say that we will never erase this and other drugs from our society. The American culture will forever have drugs as a part of it. However, without our government's leaders, an engaged society, law enforcement's watchful eye and *caring*, our society will be decimated by outrageous medical costs and a public safety nightmare rivaling the days of the early untamed West. Success in this area can only be measured a life at a time. By arresting one dealer, user, or manufacturer of a drug and then helping them to become a legitimate member of society, educating them, providing treatment for them, or ultimately punishing them and locking them up, we can control the damage to society.

This is a critical time when intervention—be it from a loved one, a concerned citizen, or the justice system—makes the difference. I have seen instances where drug users and dealers have turned their lives around, and I know each one of us has some anecdotal story where the persons involved either faced jail or getting their kids taken away from them. Most choose the right thing, some do not, and that is where we must remain vigilant.

4

Chasing the Dollar

"Money often costs too much."

— RALPH WALDO EMERSON

There are valuable tools in the tool chest of law enforcement that allow us to make the biggest impact on the criminal by seizing their ill-gotten gains and what fuels their criminal enterprise: money. Most crooks can grow more drugs, manufacture more drugs, make up Ponzi schemes, and commit other types of fraud to profit illegally, but they cannot MANUFACTURE MONEY. This is the life's blood of crime. This has however, at times, confused the reason we are in the business of law enforcement. One such tool is called the *reverse sting*. This tactic is as old as law enforcement itself and is basically the police pretending to be crooks in order to catch more crooks. Whether the police are acting as a fence receiving stolen goods and, in the process, identifying thieves, or are pretending to be selling dope and identifying drug dealers, the reverse sting is a good investigative method that identifies the major narcotic trafficker and their organization.

The biggest challenge of this legally authorized tactic is to avoid the entrapment issue that is commonly brought up as a defense. Entrapment occurs when an undercover agent crosses the line and entices the would-be criminal to commit the crime, rather than just catching them in an act of their "normal" business. An example would be offering an unusual dollar amount for the purchase of the drugs, when they command a price point more typical for the region. It would be like listing a house for $275,000 that should be sold for $500,000. Yes, a buyer will be enticed to the deal, but it screams entrapment. There is an old saying, if it sounds too good to be true, it is! I have seen the reverse sting work well in law enforcement and achieve the goal of dismantling and disrupting the criminal's business. I'll talk about such a reverse sting momentarily.

When assets are seized, the primary agency (that did the majority of the investigation) rightfully receives the majority of the assets and will equitably share with the assisting agencies. So a thousands-of-dollars seizure is substantial for the police agency, and it can mean more support for crime victims, community programs, police cars, radios, computers, and other equipment to improve police services. It is important though for the agencies involved to have proof that there was a criminal nexus and that the assets were profits of the sales of narcotics or proceeds from criminal acts. These laws are in place to protect citizens from the unlawful seizure of assets that are not direct results of criminal acts.

Understand though that agencies never *rely* on such seizures, nor can they, since they are never meant to augment budgets and they are unpredictable. However, when an investigation arises where a criminal or their enterprise has illegally profited, the law should and does allow for the seizure of identifiable assets linked to those crimes. The reinvestment of those assets to help victims, the community, and the law enforcement agency who conducted that investigation is lawful and balances the lopsided, extensive unlimited financial resources that criminals have as a result of their illegal acts. This issue is constantly under legal review with policies in place from local, state, and federal mandates.

The occasional seizure of such assets by a few law enforcement agencies that did not understand either the law or its application in these cases does not warrant the harsh penalty of abolishing the entire practice. As any action—be it legislative, judicial, or executive—is deemed questionable, it must be thoroughly reviewed before any decision is made to ignore what has historically proven to be a correct and appropriate hammer in the crime-fighting tool box. More solid prosecutions, and just as important, more meaningful punishment and deterrence is done when the criminal organization or individual is bankrupted rather than putting them in jail or taking their drugs, guns, or shell corporations away. In those instances, they return to their criminal lifestyle after a short jail sentence because their financial resources await them. Likewise, their financial resources allow them to replace whatever drugs, guns, or other assets were seized.

There was a time in the '80s and early '90s when, if a dope dealer's ill-gotten gains were seized, the police agency could acquire the dealer's exotic sports cars, weapons, etc. and press them into police service. A few agencies nationwide pushed this policy to an extreme and correctly targeted major drug dealers, but then got distracted by the seized assets. The goal of this forfeiture law is to take out the very backbone of a criminal group (their illegal assets and profits) that fuels operations and wreaks havoc in our society. If it is done only to enrich an agency, that's not right; it is corrupt and it is not what the law intended. Back then a few agencies seized assets with "Zero Tolerance" policies and their actions resulted in changes to the law. However, seizure of identifiable ill-gotten gains remains allowable (within proscribed limits and regulations) since it is immensely critical to the support of the criminal justice system.

Agencies that know best how to deploy the seizures when lawfully adjudicated are left to do so with the proper oversight from local, state, and federal guidelines. There must always be evidence and proof in order to seize such assets. Again, it is not a perfect method and no doubt mistakes are made by some, but the system is in place to help govern these actions. Law enforcement agencies should not be punished when the seizure of assets is done correctly. This has been supported by thoughtful lawmakers throughout the past few decades and the precedent has been clearly established on when such an action can take place.

After airplanes, boats, and other vehicles were seized due to a few marijuana seeds being found onboard, it became apparent that it wasn't necessarily the owner of the vehicle who had carried the contraband onboard. So the days of boats, planes, and cars being seized by agencies due to a few marijuana seeds being in the vehicle no longer occurs. Today, if police departments seize some of those Ferraris and Porsches, or other assets like homes and bank accounts, the assets are sold off only after the proper judicial adjudication to go toward the previously mentioned efforts. The law enforcement agencies do not get to keep the assets, which removes much of the temptation to abuse the laws regarding seizure of assets.

Today the laws are more reasonable and they establish strict guidelines on how to seize criminal proceeds. Both the public and law enforcement agencies are regulated from engaging and profiting from crime. So too should the criminal be regulated. This is how society should work with its law enforcement component— monitoring and adjusting the barometer as needed.

A tragedy occurred in 1990 when a Southern California police agency got caught up in the reverse sting mentality. From management on down to the undercover agent, the dollar became the focus of some investigations. I remember being on surveillance with our BNE team, conducting an investigation into the heroin trafficking activities of a group in the southeast area of Los Angeles County. While on surveillance, within blocks of the location we were watching, I saw a group of narcs (narcotic officers) in a parking lot putting away their raid gear, standing at their vehicles, wearing their police regalia. Obviously, I did not want our crooks to drive by these cops and get "burned" (compromised) if they saw this group of officers gathered in public. There was also a possibility that they were working some facet of our case. So, in order to avoid a "blue on blue" conflict (working the same suspect), I decided to meet with them.

I asked my supervisor to meet me at that parking lot so we could talk to our counterparts from this agency and let them know we were working in the area. Joe and I went over to them, introduced ourselves, and told them about our operation. They happened to be conducting surveillance on an unrelated location and on a different narcotic suspect. They said they would leave the parking lot so as not to burn our case.

That local police department detective, "Tommy" (may he rest in peace), told us he and his team were preparing for a great case next week and were going to do, and I quote him, "the mother of all reverses."

I will never forget that. Although we wished him luck and offered him any assistance needed, it was to no avail.

The following week, Tommy was killed in a gun battle over a million dollar dope deal that never transpired. I have nothing but respect for this man and his agency as he tried to do what we all do: to make our streets a little bit safer. The problems or "red flags" that appeared prior to and during the case were so apparent after the fact, that to this day it is a learning point for any investigator assigned to a narcotic unit. It is not anyone's job to second-guess this hero, but if we can learn anything from this incident and save a life, it is our duty to do so. Only then as a profession, have we have done our job.

The above incident dealt with an undercover operation where a reverse sting was being used to try and shut down a cocaine trafficking organization. During the UC meetings, things went well, entrapment was not going to be a defense, but it was the *cops* who were entrapped by the crooks. By that I mean that the crooks lured the cops into thinking they were capable of buying a million dollars' worth of cocaine. The crooks knew they had these cops distracted and strung them along, ultimately setting up an ambush. The cops became relaxed since they had done dozens of successful reverse stings before, but they forgot the basics in this case and missed the cues.

This incident has been debriefed and a lot of things have since changed the way reverse stings are done. I remember an instructor in my Special Agent academy posing a question to the class: How much dope would it take for you to take a bullet? He offered some quantities ranging from a single ounce to multi-tons. When he got to the multi-tons of drugs, an agent raised his hand. We all shook our heads in disgust including the instructor. The agent was chastised and the point was driven home: NO AMOUNT of cocaine, heroin, meth, etc. is worth taking a bullet or dying over.

After this failed sting and a few other officer-involved shootings where cops were killed in the line of duty, I was appalled by another Southern California police agency in 1999. I was supervising a narcotic task force and attended a meeting with two other law enforcement agencies regarding a conflict on an investigation. Some investigators tend to be territorial about their cases and when interest is shown by another agency into a part of their case, it's as if you are trying to burglarize their home. Usually these disputes are resolved for the greater good, with everyone realizing who has the best prosecution potential or by joining forces to combat the issue together.

This particular case was accented with the potential of huge asset forfeiture. The sergeant of the unit was unusually passionate about expressing his agency's position in this investigation. He actually became boisterous during this meeting and made a Freudian slip. When we were discussing the dismantling of the criminal enterprise and the bulk narcotic seizure that would occur, the sergeant blurted out, "Don't forget the goal of this case is to get their MONEY." He had forgotten the lesson learned earlier.

We looked at each other dumbfounded, but only for a moment, as cops tend to be a little outspoken and many I knew had a great wit. I, along with the others, gently reminded him that the goal was to make a solid case and successfully prosecute all the suspects, seize their contraband, and shut down their organization. He stared blankly at us and then realized what he had said. He got it, but he had to be reminded.

Law enforcement is grossly underfunded and goes up against these MULTI-MILLION DOLLAR criminal enterprises all the time. The taxpayer should not carry this burden, nor should the government, with its ever-tightening budgets due to difficult fiscal times. The lawful result of having a criminal organization brought to its knees by seizing their illegal profits of crime is a fitting punishment that stops the criminals dead in their tracks. Add to this that the seized assets can fund victim assistance programs, community programs, and the very police agencies that risk their lives to take on this noble task of enforcing our nation's laws responsibly. It is critical that lawful seizure, based on evidence of a crime and the reasonable standard, be allowed to continue. To leave the money in the hands of criminals only allows the death and destruction of our society to continue.

It takes courageous leadership to manage such units and organizations. The lesson must never be forgotten.

5

Leadership

"It is better to lead from behind and to put others in front,
especially when you celebrate victory when nice things occur.
You take the front line when there is danger.
Then people will appreciate your leadership.

—NELSON MANDELA

There have been numerous books written about leadership and police management. From managing a patrol shift or a correctional facility, to leading a Fortune 500 company or a large police agency, there is a plethora of information that gives various insights into this challenging world of leadership. I have seen both sides of the coin, particularly as it relates to specialized units and organizational leadership. The one factor that is a constant challenge in law enforcement is the ability to recruit, retain, and then promote qualified personnel. It takes a unique individual to join the cops in the first place, let alone to want to work an assignment like crimes against children, homicide, or narcotic enforcement. Leadership from the mid-level ranks like Special Agent supervisors, lieutenants, and sergeants is the lynch pin that sets the pace for subordinates under their command. A tone must be set at the top to show that the executives support the line and will hold the leadership accountable in both good times and bad times. A lot of valuable lessons can be learned from great leaders. Lessons can also be learned from the not-so-great leader. The singular lesson learned universally from the *not*-so-great leader is how *not* to manage.

In these difficult times of changing political winds, budget constraints, downsizing, and retirements, the attrition from law enforcement agencies across the United States is in a crisis. With the constant pendulum effect of whether to support or not to support the cops, it is always going to boil down to this: the people who work in those units, the community support and the leadership of the organization. There are plenty of books on leadership styles; one can research any of those in that genre. I offer a few instances of what happens in a law enforcement environment (and without a doubt in the private sector too) as it relates to management.

Like a professional sports team, if the coach is to be measured, one critical barometer is the team's performance. If a team is in disarray, has poor morale, lacks a winning record, or is incompetent, the coach's career is short lived. Cops are basically good folks, goal-oriented, and, because it is a paramilitary organization, follow a chain of command. Some may not care for the boss or for a particular management style, but they should always respect the rank.

Of course, leadership shouldn't be by consensus. Nor should it be a dictatorship. I have seen both styles and each is a failure. A consonance must be struck for the successful leader, along with a proven track record. This may sound simple but in reality it is a difficult technique that requires some work and a gut-check to achieve positive results.

One leadership book that I have read is called "Rules and Tools for Leaders" by Retired Major General Perry Smith. He describes a very common sense approach to effective management and leadership.[iv] The author addresses a myriad of topics applicable to several business models, military organizations, and law enforcement agencies.

When you have a group of people coming together to perform a seriously dangerous and highly specialized job, the supervisor or manager must have been able to at least do the job of those he or she supervises. Like a parent or a coach, a nurturing and mentoring yet firm approach must be taken to ensure the job gets done successfully and safely.

Lou Holtz, the famous coach of the Notre Dame football team, has also authored several books on the type of leadership needed to be successful. As one can see, the formula is out there for those who care to learn it rather than reinvent the wheel.

Over the years I saw a turnover of good, qualified personnel within several police agencies because of supervisors/managers/leaders who forced people to work the long and unusual hours inherent to this business of law enforcement all because of the case or mission, or in some instances for the leader's own ego. They disregard the fact that *people* make the job a success, not the leader. Sure, a solid leader definitely has a hand in the team's outcome, but he or she is never the sole impetus.

I have worked for and have been inspired by several outstanding supervisors, managers, and top executives who embodied the definition of leadership. Dale F, Kent W, Janette G-A, Doug O, Randy R, and Tim R are just a few, and the list thankfully goes on. I have also worked for some who were void of the necessary skill set and made me think that somewhere a village is truly missing an idiot. I remember having a meeting once with such a newly promoted manager. As the new boss, he wanted to meet with each one of his supervisors and talk about his vision for the office. I get that, and remember when I promoted, I too had a similar meeting with my management team, but my meeting went the opposite of his.

Let me explain why. He went on to *tell* me about his perceptions of my job performance and reputation, even though I never worked for him. He did not want to explain or converse about ways for improving morale, recruitment, retention, the quality of casework, or how to develop our future leaders. He bloviated about his negative perception of my supervision style and how I could improve myself by patterning myself after him. I listened, as any good cop should, to my new boss and actually wondered where he was going with this. I have dealt with many types of personalities in this job and I, along with 90 percent of the staff, were well aware of his job history and how he had landed the new position of manager. It was not the type of path most would admire. So I was actually looking forward to gaining insight into his philosophy and putting my college psych classes to work.

Anyway, he finally got to the point about how we needed to turn around the attitudes of our staff as front line supervisors. He said, "The mission comes first," and he raised his right hand to the level of his eyebrow, almost like a salute. Then he said, "and your people come second" (referring to the Special agents and non-sworn employees), and he raised his left hand to the level of his belt, which by the way was straining in holding back a physique comparable to Jabba the hut.

I remained patient and open-minded in trying to understand his philosophy. Cops in general can be very rule-oriented and sometimes they follow direction to a fault. However, when the order is illegal, immoral, or unethical, a good cop has to do the right thing and not follow such a mandate. He must speak up firmly, with conviction, and articulate his position. It can be tough, but it usually works out. Well, as one might gather, this manager had a reputation for a lack of people skills. Staff either wanted off his team or they put in transfer requests to leave the office. I now was put in the tenable position that every cop or employee eventually faces: either you are on one side of the fence or the other. It was like being back on the playground in grammar school. This time, however, I had a bit more knowledge and experience, and I was too old to play these games.

Insubordination is never a good idea, but he was looking for my explicit approval of his comment. I told him he was wrong, dead wrong. You could have heard a pin drop in that room. He looked at me with amazement, his mouth nearly wide open. It was apparent to me that he had surrounded himself with "yes" men and no one really had disagreed with him like that since he became a supervisor. I stood my ground and reminded him that _without the people, no mission could ever be accomplished_. Both the mission and the people (the employees) had to be equal and a balance has to be struck to get the best out of our organization and to serve the public trust. I next held both my hands to eye level pointing my fingers at each other to illustrate what equality looked like. No doubt, something he had forgotten years ago. Unfortunately, it was apparent to all that his philosophy was reinforced by his previous supervisor who had set the same low bar for leadership 101.

Needless to say, I was not going to be invited to his family barbecues anytime soon. We did not hit it off, and I wanted to give him some time, hoping a new change in command would be positive and he would see the good work being done by the teams in our office from a broader perspective than just his own. He did not. More good quality people left and took their valuable experience with them. This "slash and burn" or "divide and conquer" mentality of some new managers is truly juvenile.

I recognize sometimes this has to happen in corrupt and out-of-control organizations, but most times it is not necessary. Bosses like this one desire to rid the workplace of dissenting opinions and fill it with cronies or "yes" men.

A good police department's executive management eventually snares this type of individual and deals with the manager (which they did). The manager then acts as a victim and whines about how unfair he or she is being treated (which he did and quickly retired), and staff scratches their heads and says let's get back to the good work.

Another example of poor leadership occurred in the spring of 2002, when the chief of a large metropolitan Southern California police department was let go. The mayor and police commissioner would not renew their contract with him. This is their city's right and procedure as it is in most major police departments nation-wide. The chief's job is very tough and very political. He knew that but of course, the chief was not happy with the decision. Rather than accept the decision as a professional, he whined and challenged the very system that he had touted was the best—but apparently not the best for him.

The main reason cited for the nonrenewal of his contract was quite clearly reported, surprisingly enough, by the local media. Though he was an outstanding administrator, he received a vote of **no confidence** from his employees and he failed in accepting responsibility for the well-being of his workforce. His agency was losing qualified personnel at an alarming rate. People who left didn't go to higher paying cop jobs, but rather to other law enforcement agencies where they felt ***they could be treated fairly.*** Changes in leadership do happen and the incoming person must be reminded that they are accountable not only to the executives above them and to the public, but also to those under their command.

Imagine if you were running a business or you owned stock in a company where the CEO was negatively affecting the morale of the employees, the workers were leaving in droves to go work for the competition, and the company was losing money. Would you want to keep that CEO around? What do you think the stockholders and their executive board would do? I had a great boss tell me once that it's their job to block the bureaucracy of the job and buffer the BS so we could do our job. That's one good thing a leader does: he or she takes on that burden so we can take on the mission. Eric B and Jimmy B, you gentlemen are true leaders who "talk the talk and walk the walk." That is why you get the best out of your people.

In a positive change of command role, I remember an instance when a new manager arrived and met with his subordinate supervisors. This time we all sat in a room together, not separated as in the previous scenario. He discussed with us his expectations of his management team and spoke about the good work for which each of us had earned a reputation. Yes, areas for improvement were discussed but so too were the areas in which we excelled. An instant bond occurred since we realized and were told that we were in this together. We were reminded that we would be held accountable for how we supervised in both good times and bad times.

A great example of leadership at work is a case my Violent Suppression Unit conducted when solid leadership led to a successful outcome. This occurred during the investigation of a particularly violent gang member. The suspect had been on the run after carjacking an elderly woman. He was armed and dangerous and had a criminal history that included narcotics and murder. Good police work cultivated an informant who was willing to stand up and let us know the suspect's whereabouts. Once the detailed briefing was delivered by the case agent, our unit established surveillance at the apartment building. We all knew our roles, knew who would be the arrest team, the surveillance team, and the point car (the one that makes the observation and calls out when the suspect is seen), and who was handling the informant when critical information needed to be relayed to the team. Leadership does not mean distrusting your personnel and barking orders at them to follow. The role we all played was clear to each of us; and the maturity it takes for a leader to allow a team to do its job, be creative, and gain experience was evident. This was true not only from my perspective, but also from my boss, who happened to be out in the field for this operation.

When the suspect came out of the building, he was alerted to our presence and ran. The plan went down the toilet, but the fail-safe is we are trained to be flexible and adapt to such scenarios. In this case, it ended up being the supervisor (myself) and my boss pursuing the suspect. I was in a Ford Mustang parked on the street as the suspect ran past me. I put the car in reverse and followed him for about half a block, then executed a customary 180-degree spin so I could be in drive and continue with the chase. My boss, who was in foot pursuit, now had the suspect cornered as he tried to climb a tall gate in front of another apartment building. I jumped out of my car to assist in the foot pursuit. As the suspect climbed up the fence, he threw his gun away, knowing that we were about to encounter him. We had our guns trained on him and ordered him down off the fence. To his credit, he listened, followed the order, and was quickly handcuffed.

The suspect was placed into custody without incident and booked at the city jail. Afterward, our team held our customary debriefing session. This is when we all have an adult conversation and talk about what we did right, what we did wrong, and most importantly, what can we improve on so we don't make the same mistakes the next time out. I guided the dialog to make sure everyone had input. Even my boss, who occasionally joined us in our field enforcement operations, participated in the conversation, but he let me, and more importantly LET US, have the necessary conversations. He practiced what he preached and set an example for all of us to follow.

I'd like to return your attention to the initial meeting my boss, Dale, had with his management team in his office prior to this mission. He added to his statement that he would ultimately accept responsibility for our actions since he was our boss. That showed me the fortitude and courage needed to be a good leader. His leadership and friendship will always be appreciated by me and by all those who worked with him as he brought an esprit de corps and a breath of fresh air to this sometimes off-the-charts business of ours. Thank you, Dale.

6

Signs and Pot

*"All truths are easy to understand once they are discovered.
The point is to discover them"*

— GALILEO GALILEI

Thus far, I have shared many of my law-enforcement experiences related to drugs, drug users, drug dealers, and even drug manufacturers. Now I'd like to take some time to share with you a few facts related to drugs of which the general public should be aware. These facts sometimes state the obvious and do not glamorize the experience that pro-legalization advocates would have one believe. Crime reduction efforts pale relative to a war.

The United States is currently mustering a gallant effort to fight a war on terrorism that struck our country in New York on September 11, 2001. We have virtually authorized *carte blanche* to find these barbarians who attacked us and hand deliver justice to them to protect our nation. Our Democratic president who took over this war from the previous Republican administration has ramped up this attack by firing missiles from drones 30,000 feet in the skies above a foreign country to assassinate those we SUSPECT of preparing to do us harm. No protests or demonstrations by activists claiming innocent lives are at risk, no demands for body cameras, grand jury proceedings, arrests, or "stop and frisk" issues—just pure and simple executions at the tip of a missile. That is war.

But our "war on drugs" isn't really a war—we are fighting crime. If some currently illegal drugs can be used as medicine, I gladly support that use, as long as the science and research is behind it. I recommend we treat medicine as the important subject it is, and not as the farce pro-legalization zealots want with no government interference or regulation, just the right and ability to manufacture drugs anytime, anywhere. We have rules when it comes to our food, the water supply, and alcohol manufacturing, and drugs should be at least as important as any of these. Let's keep terrorists and criminals from getting rich on the backs of addicts, the poor, and the elite. Let's be intellectually honest: legalization is not the answer, nor is total incarceration. We have to strike a balance. I, for one, do not want the government or cartels to manage the "commodity" of drugs. Both have proven to be inept and unreliable in these matters. Government can barely manage our educational systems, its own corruption, universal health care, and the economy. And cartels are no better than the terrorists. Do you really think our government can successfully handle the multitrillion dollar international drug trade with drug cartels and terrorists as their business partners?

We then return to the badge-carrying members of police agencies who enforce the laws of our land, including narcotic laws. Society seems to wrestle with its soul on this issue, sometimes in favor of politics, race, color, and creed. As we have seen, drugs have always been tolerated in our society, joked about, and even glamorized—until it hits a loved one or someone we know. Terrorists use the drug trade to support their evil mandates. There are cases across the United States like the 2004 case in San Diego, California, that netted several suspects selling heroin in order to buy Stinger missiles for al-Qaida[v]. If this is not a clear example that drug money is directly linked to terrorism, I don't know what is.

Short-term memories affect our perception of how perverse the drug problem really is. In cases where an individual suffers from mental illness, the abuse of drugs or alcohol exacerbates the condition. We are reminded of it when the rich and famous—like Cory Monteith ("Glee" actor, died of a heroin and alcohol overdose), Phillip Seymour Hoffman (actor, died of heroin overdose), Elvis Presley (The "King," died of prescription drug overdose including barbiturates and codeine), Michael Jackson (pop star, died of overdose of propofol and anti-anxiety medications), Kurt Cobain (rock star of Nirvana, had a lethal dose of heroin in his system, then put a shotgun to his head and committed suicide), Chris Farley (comedic actor, died of cocaine and morphine overdose), Whitney Houston (singer, died of overdose of cocaine and using alcohol with Xanax), and Amy Winehouse (singer, died of acute alcohol poisoning)—make the evening news. The average citizen gets no headline.

Only when it touches their personal lives do people want to rid this scourge of addiction, but they are still afraid to have the real conversation that alcohol, illicit drugs, and abused prescription drugs are dangerous. These famous people are memorialized as celebrities and great people, but they were also ***addicts***. Say it like it is. Race and wealth, social status and income do not know boundaries when it comes to addiction. To treat these substances as a harmless recreational distraction by talented entertainers or curious kids degrades the gift of life and ignores the threat. We glamorize the addict's fame when we should be honestly critical of them and point out what got them hooked and how to prevent others from landing on that coroner's slab.

Here are some common-sense, quick facts on how drugs get into your system, how long they last, and what effects occur in the body. Keep as a reference some of these basic signs to look for in a loved one, a friend, or someone you care about that might be using/abusing drugs.

<u>The following are what we call in police work, "clues":</u>

- A drug can be taken via external or internal means, including snorting, smoking, orally, or intravenously. It enters the bloodstream, goes to the brain, and saturates the receptor sites located in the brain.
- The fastest way into the body is by intravenous injection (iv), sniffing, smoking, or placing the drug under the tongue. These methods take about 2–5 minutes to get the drug into your body.
- Injection under the skin or into muscle takes about 5–15 minutes to enter the bloodstream.
- Oral use, like a pill or liquid, takes the drug about 15–60 minutes to take effect.
- A continuous method is via a patch, iv, or implant.
- Being under the influence involves a mild effect on the brain's receptors with physiological signs such as

un-coordination; changes in blood pressure, pulse rate, or pupil size; mood change; and distorted time and visual perception

- Toxic effects pose a severe impairment of normal body functions such as psychosis, hallucinations, violence, tremors, coma, paranoia, and disorientation.

<u>Following is a brief list of biochemicals found in the body that drug use will activate and then deplete.</u> I have also included what the biochemical effect is on the body when using certain types of drugs.

- <u>Endorphins</u>—Pain relief, endurance, euphoric feelings, and control of blood pressure. (Occurs when heroin, marijuana, or PCP is used.)
- <u>Dopamine</u>—Muscle tone, stimulation, energy, motivation, appetite, attention span, pleasure. (Occurs when nicotine, caffeine, cocaine, or methamphetamines are used.)
- <u>Serotonin</u>—Mental stability, appetite, sleep control, self-esteem, and discipline. (Occurs when alcohol, nicotine, cocaine, or PCP is used.)
- <u>Acetylcholine</u>—Memory, learning, reflexes. (Occurs when marijuana or nicotine is used.)
- <u>Cortisone</u>—Immune system, healing, stress control. (Occurs when heroin, anabolic steroids, or cocaine is used.)
- <u>Insulin</u>—Energy, glycogen storage, blood sugar control. (Occurs when heroin, cocaine, methamphetamines, or marijuana is used.)

Rave parties often act as fashionable events in which teens and college-age kids participate. In all the deaths associated with overdoses from drugs like ecstasy, ketamine (also known as "Special K," which is an anesthesia and antidepressant), and a host of other designer drugs that compare to methamphetamine and LSD, there are some common denominators. These are noted by emergency room physicians who routinely pronounce death on these uninformed kids who think they are being "cool."

<u>Some signs to look for are:</u>

- If the kid passes out, this is serious. **Unconsciousness is a sign**. Don't make the fatal mistake, as one parent did, of assuming that a kid just passed out due to drunkenness. In many cases of unconsciousness, the high school student dies the next morning. If you care about the person, find out what they were doing just before they passed out. Ask the friend they were with. Even if you find no evidence that alcohol or pills were ingested, **rush** the unconscious kid to an emergency room. Better to be embarrassed than to bury a child.
- If the person experiences sudden and uncontrollable vomiting, followed by passing out, get him or her to the hospital or call 911.
- If you see heavy, profuse sweating, it could be a sign of drug use. Some drugs dehydrate the body. The party promoters will actually shut off the water at a concert venue or dance club in order to sell bottled water at triple the price because they know the people will pay anything to drink water during their drug-induced night of dancing. The drug dealer, I mean the promoter, makes money and the coroner's office gets to keep someone's son or daughter in a freezer.

- Watch for delirium or hallucinating. This is a MAJOR sign; DO NOT IGNORE IT! Get medical attention immediately.

The above observations, in and of themselves, indicate that something is WRONG. Sure you can explain away some of the symptoms to being drunk or a high from a marijuana cigarette, but it is an incredible gamble on a human life. A common theme of family and friends who lost loved ones when drugs were involved is some of the above observations being made just prior to them dying. This is particularly true when the victim was at a party where it was obvious that drugs and booze were available.

During the past decade, several kids died at such parties. On a local talk radio station, I heard a grieving mother describe how her daughter, a high school honor student, went to such a party, threw up several times during the evening, then crashed at a friend's house. The friend (some friend, huh?) told the parent at the house that her pal was sleeping off the effects from a wild party. The uninformed parent went along with that excuse. A few hours later, when they tried to wake the dead girl up, it was too late. If you are going to host drunken kids at your house, you are not only remiss in your responsibility as a parent for allowing it, you also are obligated to help them get medical attention if you see one passing out. Don't forget the liability issue too. Their death or drunk driving accident is on you since you were serving them or allowing them to drink.

Another story recounts a college student who took some drugs and began hallucinating. His friends thought it was funny. Then he passed out. They rushed him to a local hospital and dropped him off anonymously on the doorstep of the emergency room, like an unwanted newborn. An hour later he was dead. The kids were later caught and told of their friend's death. I hope they learned something from this tragedy. The goal of any college student should be to graduate, alive. There are hundreds of stories like these, including the observations of the emergency room doctors who routinely treat overdoses.

Getting back to rave parties: Since the type of drugs ingested at these events slows the respiratory system, an artificial airway often must be made to assist the victim in breathing. This simple life-saving technique has saved some, but the key is getting help early before unconsciousness settles in. Parents and kids both need to know that in addition to yourself, it is OK to care about the health of those around you, even if you think they are just casual users of drugs.

Just ask the state of Colorado, whose emergency room visits are skyrocketing after their uninformed voters decided to legalize marijuana in that state in 2014. Keep a cautious eye out for this state, as the marijuana issue looks to me to have been a scam the public and its government bought into, and now its people are getting hurt. Meanwhile, the cartels and crooks are getting rich off the misery. I believe most states will recognize this and fight pro-legalization efforts.

Talk to your kids, friends, and family members, and be honest about drugs. It's nauseating when I hear politicians or professional men and women in today's world and workforce say things like, "I did it and I turned out OK" or "It just made me feel good and I really did have a good time" or "I didn't hurt anyone; we just got stoned and had the munchies." These and other comments like them only trivialize the dangers and encourage our youth who might be at that crossroad to try drugs rather than steer clear of them. So what happens? You now have kids saying, "Mom and Dad did it and they turned out OK, then probably I will too." This is the absolute wrong message to be sending out.

A drug that irresponsible people still feel is OK is pot, or marijuana. Know this though: the typical marijuana joint has over 100 known carcinogens. That is like smoking a pack of cigarettes in one sitting. OK, you can do that, but now add the chemical/drug THC to this product. This is not your uncle's pot from the '60s. THC, or tetrahydrocannabinol, is the main chemical that gets you high in marijuana. Current studies show that today's cannabis is at least four (4) times more potent than in past decades. At least right now, it is still a schedule I narcotic and illegal under federal law. There's a reason for that; but some of our legislators are high themselves and forget about why it is scheduled as such.

Marijuana, contrary to some beliefs, is not harmless and should NOT be legalized. It's strong enough to be considered a medicine. It is a billion dollar industry, with drug cartels and organized crime entrenched in it. Criminal organizations commit murder and other crimes against people and the environment to grow it and sell it. Growers set up deadly booby traps to protect their illegal marijuana gardens in the national forests, as I saw firsthand when conducting eradication missions early on in my BNE career. They dump the toxic waste from the chemicals used to grow marijuana into the natural environment, thus poisoning the natural habitat.

I've yet to see the big pharmaceutical companies issue a murder contract or conduct a takeover robbery and kill the clerks working in the store over nasal spray. Yet the marijuana industry is plagued with violent crimes like this. Every day, dispensaries are under attack from local gang members and other criminals since they are a cash-only business and attract the drug addict, not the individual dying from cancer. However, some ignorant people still say, "It's just pot, no one gets really hurt." Murders routinely happen at these "dispensaries". Drugs are a violent crime, period.

If some people believe that it should be legalized for medicinal purposes like Vicodin, penicillin, or codeine (to name a few of legitimate drugs used to treat various types of infections and pain), then let it be approved by the American Medical Association. Have a ringing endorsement from the majority of physicians in this country blessing it, and add approval from the Food and Drug Administration to make it legal. Then it will have status as a true medicine, accepted by all, and prescribed by REAL doctors, not just a "caregiver" who never set foot in medical school and looks like he graduated from the high school in the movie *Fast Times at Ridgemont High.*

Also, do you really think that if pot had those medical qualities, like aspirin and some other medicines, that some major medical corporation wouldn't have already marketed it and made billions like the other pharmaceutical companies? The reason is hasn't happened is that it is too easily abused and the criminal markets will never give up their involvement with the addict. The crooks won't suddenly turn over a new leaf and say, "now that it is legal, we have to stop our life of crime and turn legit." That is BS. Another misleading statement I have heard people say is: "I just smoke a little bit, in the privacy of my house, and I'm OK."

Well, you are the exception. In January 2003, I watched Barbara Walters interview the talented singer-entertainer Whitney Houston and her husband, Bobby Brown. At the time, their daughter was a child and I thought what a wonderful role model Houston and her husband would be to a little girl. Then she and her husband admitted to using marijuana "occasionally" and felt it was not a big deal. I said to myself then, "I think that family is going have some issues." Mr. Bobby Brown said he uses it "every other day" because he suffers from a medical condition. They admitted their daughter knows about it and she is OK with it. Whitney Houston did not think it was such a big deal because it's only marijuana.

Really?

Meanwhile, Whitney Houston got arrested at an airport for smuggling the stuff, and her husband was in the news for being in and out of jail for drug use and drunk driving. Years later, this beautiful, talented lady with a one-in-a-million voice, tragically died of an overdose in a hotel bathtub. Their daughter also fought with drug use then sadly Mr. Brown did an interview in January 2015 talking about this tragic chain of events. Again, this is a clue in police work and shows the American public why they should not support legalization, even if they think that "it's only pot" and "no one ever really gets hurt." Well, its painfully obvious, people do get hurt.

Again, I go back to my experiences over the past decades as a cop. I saw firsthand that marijuana is a drug that every drug addict and most criminals have tried early on in their criminal experimentation. It is the beginning of addictive and criminal behavior. Does this resonate with anyone? Are these responsible adults over 21, with successful personal and professional lives, who only want to be left alone in the privacy of their own home to smoke an occasional joint?

I am empathetic to those who are addicted and trying to fight their dependency, or those who suffer from terminal diseases and are searching for any help that's available. The concept for a limited relaxed sanction for marijuana was intended and supported by California voters to be a COMPASSIONATE ACT for those who are really sick. I agree with that proposition.

But this somehow got perverted into legalizing it with little control of dispensing it. I can't go to my local grocery store and buy morphine, Vicodin, or amoxicillin, so why did this caring approach to get medicinal marijuana out there become like buying ice cream from a local store whenever you want it? *Shame on society and on our legislators and politicians who fell asleep at the wheel on this one.*

I support programs that work, that save people from total addiction and return them to a productive, healthy, and legal life. Sure some of society's elite and part of the entertainment industry or very wealthy and famous people claim it's no big deal; but their actions speak louder than words when arrest after arrest occurs and their careers and lives, and the lives of their families, are shattered and publicly ridiculed. Yes, money and fame can buy drugs, but it doesn't buy class.

If you have tried drugs and survived, be fair to those you speak to and paint the other half of the picture. For every person who says they actually enjoyed their time when they smoked a little pot or did a harder drug—OK, maybe that was their experience. Bullshit. I know those people also know of the darker and more painful side to drug use that affected someone close to them. All I ask is that they just be honest. The person you may be speaking to may be your child, nephew, niece, sibling, coworker, an impressionable young person, or friend. You can mention those comments like the above but also tell them that you realize you were lucky and intelligent by making the choice to move on with your life so as not to become an addict or an embarrassment to a family, or to build an arrest record or worse.

Don't encourage them, educate them.

Lots, and I do mean lots, of people can't break the use of drugs, and they become criminals, addicts, sick, or die. Sometimes they kill others as a result of their habit. Examples are bountiful. Just look at the news or do an Internet search on this topic. On January 15, 2015, the Monroe Police Department in Michigan arrested a 37-year-old woman who had overdosed in the bathroom of a McDonald's restaurant. The kicker is that her two daughters, one nine years old and the other five years old, were the ones that found her passed out in the bathroom and ran out screaming. Officers arrived and found the woman unconscious and slumped over the toilet. The typical accoutrements were next to her: a syringe and burnt spoon that heated the heroin to be injected. Child protective services arrived and cared for the kids, and now another family is ruined (Monroe News, Wednesday, January 28, 2015).

People should scream with outrage. This was not an accident. It is not an accident when you put drugs or booze in your system and then get behind the wheel of a 3,000-pound vehicle to drive the streets of America with your kids inside the car. It is dead wrong. Society needs to remain alert to this problem and discourage drug use. Tell anyone who is curious about it, that it is illegal. Don't glamorize its use with nostalgia. Let's get the media to help since they can reach a larger audience. I'm sure most of us have seen the smoking commercial, depicting a woman whose chronic smoking habit led to her throat cancer and she now has a stoma. Pretty graphic, but it drives the point home. The recreational pot smokers should play that commercial every time they consider lighting up a joint.

Be fair when talking about drugs. The key is TALKING intelligently about it with the facts. Too many times, we react too late when a loved one is hurt or killed. The time to deal with its experimentation is before the tragedy.

Another story that drives the point home (no pun intended) stems from an incident in August 2014 in Pennsylvania. A retired teacher and his wife had pulled to the shoulder of Highway 81. He was changing a flat tire when he was struck and killed by the suspect. The day of the crash, the suspect told state troopers he had smoked marijuana the day before and blacked out just before the crash.

After a blood test, police found a significant amount of marijuana (THC) in his bloodstream. This impairment led to the accident. The suspect was charged with third degree murder, homicide by vehicle and while DUI, and operating a vehicle under the influence of marijuana.

The argument I hear that revenue will be generated and states can balance their budgets and put money into education is more BS. I've yet to see the money roll into the State's coffers and the school systems across this nation are still in need of help. The marijuana industry with its wave of crime is not the answer. Let's pay attention to the signs, we just might save some lives.

7

Bullshit that Cops Put Up With

"You can observe a lot just by watching."

— Yogi Berra

This might be the most controversial chapter in this book as it deals with the raw experience only known to those in our profession. Working as a narcotic agent and a front line police officer provides a perspective of human behavior every time a cop interacts with the public. I must admit I have arrested both minorities and white people. I have arrested doctors, lawyers, teachers, business persons, gang members, homeless folks, actors, Hollywood industry executives, juveniles, elderly people, men, and women. Sadly, I have even arrested police officers. I have had to place 72-hour-mental-health holds on people who I determined were a danger to themselves or others, and check them into a mental health facility for treatment. When investigating crime and enforcing our country's laws, equal opportunity applies to every race, religion, and status in society. This business is color-blind and knows no limits in the range of humanity that breaks the law or those that need help.

The Officer Down Memorial Page (ODMP)[vi] documents the deaths of cops that are killed every year in the line of duty. Recent statistics have shown an increase in ambushes and unprovoked attacks on police, which has prompted a new study from the national law enforcement officers killed in the line of duty organization called LEOKA (Law Enforcement Officers Killed and Assaulted). The study will include the unique perspectives of ambush victims and perpetrators. The study, due out in 2016, is reviewing cases from as far back as 1995, looking for general themes of offender motives and officer perceptions.

According to the National Law Enforcement Officers Memorial Fund (NLEOMF), every 58 hours an American police officer is killed in the line of duty[vii]. On average, about 130 cops die in the line of duty every year in the United States. These officers either were murdered or died while doing their job. I, along with my peers, attend several funerals every year for coworkers who are taken too soon. This is a very sobering part of the job. There are no race, gender, or status issues at these funerals; we all wear a badge.

So where else can you bad-mouth your government, speak in public venues about religion and race issues, pass local ordinances legalizing drugs, stage protests, walk the streets after midnight, not step on a land mine on your way home, burn your country's flag, or jump in a car and travel around the country without having to bribe local border patrols to keep you safe? In America, you can buy a gun at your local sporting goods store, buy drugs if you want, and run for any political office. Our country is unique and cannot be compared to others where cops don't carry guns. It's like comparing apples to oranges. Contrast this to life in China or the

Middle East, where there is little crime. That's because they jail political dissenters and execute or amputate limbs from robbers, burglars, and murderers. How about public canings like in India? I sure didn't see any protestors there with signs calling for death of the government officials or police; or the publishing of home addresses of the cops involved in an incident; or the wanton burning and looting of innocent, hard-working, city business owners because of a negative contact with police or a perception of a social injustice.

This is classic on how most of the public perceives our actions, or inaction, without considering the totality of the circumstance. Consider the 2014 Ferguson incident, where a police officer shot and killed an unarmed man. The media then exploited the racial angle (though ultimately the officer was exonerated of any wrong doing by the Federal Department of Justice, and found to be acting within his lawful scope of duties). With every situation where cops take serious measures to protect themselves or the public, the event must be initially viewed through the eyes of the first responder. The first responder is the cop out there on the beat who is responding to a call from the public they serve to check out a local robber or criminal up to no good. He or she is the one who has to deal with often radical and unpredictable circumstances that are thrust upon them as part of the job.

Now I know how I was taught to behave in society as a young man. My father taught me not to be scared of the police, as long as I was doing the right thing. I did not get the talk that it was OK to go ahead and "take on" the cops, be disrespectful, throw rocks at them or light their police cars on fire, steal from others, or smoke a little pot and then fight with the cops, being sure to go for their gun but later say you didn't mean to act that way. If I robbed a local store in my hometown, my dad would have kicked my behind and turned me over to the authorities, and I would have faced the consequences. Cops do not, and never will, put up with criminal behavior—nor should a democratic society.

A couple of recent tragedies drive this point home. In October 2014, a Sacramento deputy sheriff was shot and killed as he and another deputy investigated a suspicious vehicle in a parking lot. A male occupant of the vehicle opened fire on the deputies with an AR-15 military assault rifle. He was instantly killed and the suspects fled. They then carjacked a vehicle and shot two more officers before they were captured.

In September 2014, two Pennsylvania state troopers were ambushed by a white supremacist during a late night shift change at their barracks, leaving one officer dead and another wounded. After an intensive manhunt, the killer was brought to justice and is now going through the court process. The governor of that state, Tom Corbett, said in response, "Every attack on an officer of the law is an attack on our state, our country and civilized society. The incident in Blooming Grove shows, once again, that our first responders face constant danger in order that the rest of us may live in peace and safety."[viii]

Don't kid yourself; when society relaxes its views towards crime and drugs, it is the police that will be the first line of defense and the first victims. Look at what is happening overseas. Terrorists are murdering street cops with wanton disregard. The January 2015 attack in France where an illustrator of a local newspaper was assassinated also resulted in the cold-blooded murder of a female French police officer who was standing on the street doing her job, alone. (I will say it again: in my humble observation, cops should *always* have a partner right next to them.)

Another overseas incident involved the all-too-common tactic intended to intimidate the population from becoming police officers. The cowardly tactic is to send gunmen to police academies or police stations to shoot it up or blow it up. In March of 2014, in Karachi, Pakistan, four police officers were shot to death in their barracks[ix]. The police are told by their management to put on their uniforms at the station to avoid being readily identified as a cop going to and from work. They are under constant attack by gangs and terrorists. (Another reason it's called a safety retirement.)

Don't think this is unique to the Middle East. In January 2015, a man opened fire on police attending a swearing-in ceremony for new officers in New Hope, Minnesota. Yes, the state of Minnesota in the United States. Two officers were shot before police returned fire and killed the man. The officers are expected to survive. In June 2015, a man drove up to the Dallas Police Department in an armored car and shot up the police station before he was killed by Police.

Notice I have not beleaguered the point of race or age involving the suspects mentioned in the incidents chronicled throughout this book. It is intentional because, to the dismay of the general mood of the country, these suspects were a mixed bag of white, Latino, black, old, and young. Again, crime is an equal opportunity employer to those who choose it and does not discriminate. All lives matter.

So I do say it is bullshit that one race or ethnicity feels somehow singled out by local, state, or federal law enforcement. The reality is this: more minorities are killed by other minorities or criminals than at the hands of cops. Other than our military, what job can you think of that puts its employees in harm's way? By "harm's way" I mean a situation where people want to hurt you because of your chosen profession. Cops wear a uniform and represent authority, or represent a criminal's ticket back to prison where they do not want to go. Being a cop means there is a very real chance that certain people want to kill you.

We sign up for that and know that. The public and our politicians sometimes forget that.

I've participated in the court system, and I respect the laws of the land and our Constitution, like the fact that grand jury proceedings are supposed to be kept secret so innocent and frightened witnesses and victims can have a voice to be heard. I may not agree with the outcome at times, but it is our nation's system. But how was it OK for a major media outlet to publish the personal home address of one of the person's involved in a sensitive grand jury process, knowing that person is the subject of the inquiry with pending death threats and that he happens to be a police officer?

It was somehow all right to put the officer's professional life and personal life under the microscope in public, but the suspect is protected like a saint. Out of equality, I think it has to work both ways. Truly there is no such thing as a fair fight. How about we delve into the suspect's life and family's life, how he was brought up, what kind of student he or she was, who he or she hung out with, and whether he or she had scrapes with the law before. Did the suspect have any prior convictions for crimes committed? And how about publishing the suspect's home address in case anyone wants to know? Leave race out of it; focus on the behavior, not the color.

Even after facts are reported and testified to, some people continue the lie of racism or brute force only to satisfy a headline. They do this to stir up negative emotions to further a political viewpoint rather than reporting the truth of the matter. In the Ferguson case, the Grand jury witnesses, including minorities, medical professionals, and the police, determined that the Ferguson shooting just flat out did not happen as the media and others initially reported. The belief that the suspect was putting his hands up when he was shot was proven to be absolutely false. But I see millionaires, specifically professional athletes, wearing T-shirts memorializing the event and raising their hands up on national television to evoke a visceral response from the public. I think that is about as ignorant as it gets. Again, money and status don't buy class or intellectual honesty.

The use of force during deadly confrontations is often unbelievably charged with emotions, adrenaline and fear. It is constantly under the microscope by all to judge the officers and determine if they went out-of-bounds in those critical seconds or minutes of an incident. Most of the time, the police get it right. When they do get it wrong, then of course the full throttle of justice should be meted out, and it is. Cops will get a harsh sentence, lose their pensions, and never work in the industry they dedicated their life to if they are found guilty. It has to be this way because we are entrusted with the public's faith and mandated to enforce the law and protect the community. I feel that same level of scrutiny should be applied when a suspect is in the wrong.

Contrary to popular belief, the police do get training—and a lot of it. I have seen times when we were trained never to go "hands on" with a suspect since that would equalize the playing field and the suspect could get the upper hand in a life-and-death struggle. That's why we used tools such as batons, Tasers, and tear gas to keep a suspect at arms distance at all times. Then training adjusted in later decades and it now teaches grappling techniques and ground fighting since most fights end up going to the pavement. Now there are increasing problems with that approach, so it may revert to avoiding the wrestling match altogether by using other devices to stun or stop a suspect.

When I look at incidents such as LAPD or the NYPD officers applying a choke hold, I know it's "damned if you do, damned if you don't." If an officer hits the suspect with a baton, mace, Taser, or anything but going "hands on" and the suspect lives, it is deemed excessive force and too brutal of a tactic. Then if we swarm a suspect with bodies piled up on him and go "hands on" to apply a choke hold or other restraint, without using batons or guns or Tasers, it is deemed excessive. Damned if we do, damned if we don't.

Well, in the infamous LAPD incident that ignited city wide riots, officers pursued a suspect demonstrating all the signs of being under the influence of drugs. The LAPD officers fired a Taser at the suspect and he pulled the darts out. Remember that drugs often give users an imperviousness to pain and seemingly super strength. Next the officers tried to swarm him, using their sheer body weight to tackle him to the ground. He threw all of them off. So all that was left was to shoot him or strike him with batons. The officers consciously decided not to kill him and to use baton strikes, which their department allowed at that time to gain compliance from a combative suspect. Yes, it may seem ugly to those who have never faced a situation more dangerous and stressful than standing in a long line to get a flavored coffee drink, but sometimes it is better to use force that doesn't result in killing somebody. That fight lasted about a minute and 16 seconds. That's it. One minute and 16 seconds. After all the trials and reviews and Monday morning quarterbacking, the federal judge in the case ruled that only in the *last few seconds,* where approximately 6 or so baton strikes occurred, were the baton strikes that were out of policy.

So there you have it: mere seconds on a grainy video, in the middle of the night, looked at over and over again, over the course of months in front of a national audience with a race card thrown in. That's what got those cops convicted and a criminal set free. The rest is history.

Add to this the infamous video spread through various media outlets and social media sites. Now if you were to have a body camera and dashboard camera footage of the entire event, it would have told a different story. But it would still be a very ugly story on how the reality of violent confrontations with police by intoxicated, belligerent ex-convicts in the commission of a crime happens every day on our nation's streets. Yes, I welcome the technology for this generation and future generations of cops, but it needs to (and should) work both ways. It will tell the real story of what happened, and only a part of the entire story. The cop or the citizen may be vindicated with technology, but we still can't rely on it as 100 percent of the evidence. It never will be. Here is why:

Ever heard the saying, "Be careful what you wish for"? I will use a sausage analogy: It tastes great, and it can be enjoyed as a meal or as an appetizer. But have you ever seen sausage being made? It's not a pretty picture.

Body cameras are not a panacea. They can only reveal a one-dimensional view of an event, from a slice of an angle. Audio helps, but it is nothing like physically being there. Standing in a dimly lit alley, listening to the inflection of a voice, sensing a suspect's defiant attitude, looking at the eyes of a deranged suspect, feeling that first grip or punch, smelling booze on someone's breath, seeing bloodshot eyes or dilated pupils, observing a suspect's body language, seeing beads of sweat on their forehead or a perspiration-stained shirt, and observing the total rage of someone getting ready to fight you because they think they are immune from lawful police contact. These are the things that will never be truly captured on a body camera or audio device. Multiple events and quick movements unfold in split seconds. The officer and witnesses are needed to corroborate such an event, particularly when there is a fatal outcome that took a few seconds to arrive at (according to a body camera). And those few seconds felt like a lifetime for the cop out there risking his or her life—all for what could have just been a ticket or a warning.

What will the public want next? Perhaps they'll demand that officers launch a drone overhead in the air on every contact with the public so it can be recorded like a Super Bowl game? I predict the body cameras will infuriate people just as often as they may exonerate an officer because the public will get a glimpse of the chaos that cops are routinely exposed to.

Let's go back to the topic of officer training. I suggest that in addition to training law enforcement officers, the PUBLIC and our LEGISLATORS/POLITICIANS should also be trained. Just like the police officer is trained in dealing with the public, the public should be trained to obey the laws and to conduct themselves professionally when dealing with situations involving the police. The first day of what I would call "community-based citizen sensitivity training" should have a few key lessons like: "A law enforcement officer is allowed to speak with you, especially when someone called them to check your well-being or that of others. So listen, be courteous, and be respectful." Cops have to abide by this lesson, so too should the public.

Another lesson might be: "Remember that police are allowed to give lawful orders in the performance of their duties, so compliance is all that is being asked." Are we really so backwards in our thinking that in 2015, America shudders when a uniformed police officer approaches them? That is bullshit.

I'm guessing people learned this fear or dislike of cops from fearful, ignorant, racist, and misinformed persons who wish to perpetuate rebellion over an imagined grievance. I never instigated the behavior when I encountered violent resistance, passive resistance, or verbal abuse from a citizen or suspect that I contacted. I have better things to do than to pick a fight with people I don't know, and risk getting hurt or missing out on time with family and friends. Cops have a job to do and it is really too bad that some folks feel anxiety over it. How do they think we feel? It is a mutual cost shared by all Americans living in this country, so we should all be engaged in the process.

Consider the March 2015 LAPD shooting of a transient on skid row. Of course, the typical slander and accusations against the police made quick headlines. Reporting like, "Unarmed Black Man Shot by White Cops" was the immediate story. Snippets of video were released and the armchair quarterbacking began. Facebook posts by the general public screamed "Here we go again." (And in most cases, it was true—here we went again bashing cops who, most of the time, are found innocent once the facts are played out.)

The transient shot in this case was a convicted bank robber who had just been released from prison. He had a false identity and was selling narcotics from tent to tent on skid row. He swung at the police, then nearly ripped a gun out of one of the cops' holsters. The officer (who happened to be an African American) drew his weapon and gave multiple verbal commands for the suspect to stop the attack. The suspect failed to do so. The officer then shot and killed the bad guy, I mean the suspect. This is not rocket science. It happens in the blink of an eye. Cops have to make this call instantly, digesting a set of circumstances while exposed to a physical attack, and they have to make the *right* call. That officer did. Then the media finds out that the officer is an African American and the circumstances of the shooting are clear and justified. The press gets bored of the story, anarchists are unable to inspire any racist angle, so the story quietly fades away. Cameras and recordings show only a peek into what the circumstances truly were.

In my experience, the use of force—whether it came from my baton, a control hold, or the pointing of my gun at someone—always resulted from the suspect's behavior. Period. When a suspect decides to lead cops on a dangerous vehicle pursuit through city streets, or when a suspect is in the commission of a crime, or when he decides to fight with a police officer, then the proper reaction by a trained professional is warranted and legal.

Now fast forward to the aftermath protests resulting from the Ferguson, Missouri shooting incident. The stepfather yelled at a crowd that was at a fever pitch after a verdict they did not like was announced. He yelled to the crowd to do the wrong thing by stating, and I quote, "Burn this bitch down, burn this bitch down." Yes, this is an emotional and volatile situation. The crowd was standing in an open lot and the media said that because they were emotional, it was somehow understandable to react this way. Well, in my 30-year career and in how I was trained, taught, and raised, this is called inciting a riot. All the respected civil rights leaders I admire—Martin Luther King, President Kennedy, and Ghandi to name a few—advocate nonviolent measures when conducting a protest. Could you imagine any one of these leaders standing up in front of a crowd, yelling what Michael Brown's stepfather yelled, then condoning the total destruction of property belonging to innocent business owners in the very same community in which they live?

Then an absolute insult to decency occurred in mid-December 2014 after another such protest. These were the chants of protestors as they walked the streets of New York after a few people disagreed with another legal process and decision and caused a public uproar. This protest too did not follow what a true civil rights leader would call for. Instead, the group was allowed to walk in protest—blocking traffic and law-abiding citizens from travelling the roadways—and yell *"What do you want? Dead Cops! When do you want it? Now!"*

What was the result of this protest? One week later, two NYPD police officers were assassinated in cold blood, in their patrol car eating lunch. What other career has that kind of absolute horror when simply taking a lunch break or doing your job? The disingenuous comparison of criminals being contacted by the police and it turning fatal for the suspects because they are in the commission of a crime to cops doing their lawful job and who are men and women from the community, supporting their families is not right. One of the officers killed, NYPD Officer Ramos, was even about to become an ordained deacon. I happen to agree with U.S. Attorney General Holder on one thing: On December 1, 2014, Holder was speaking to a group of leaders at the White House. In commenting on the Ferguson shooting in reference to law enforcement, he said, "Police too have the right to come home."

So I ask, what American city—or any city in the world—would allow a group of people to walk down its streets and chant something like, **"What do you want, DEAD? ... (fill in the blank by saying "DEAD" whatever race, public official, or religious group you want) ... "When do you want it? Now!"**

This kind of rhetoric must never be tolerated. Never. That is not what the First Amendment is about. To support this type of hateful and inflammatory language and actions, and to incite death onto a group of people is, as I mentioned in an earlier chapter, illegal, immoral, and unethical.

Speak up. Speak against this type of thinking, especially when it encourages such violent action against the very people who are charged with protecting the public and keeping the peace. Of course words did not kill the two NYPD officers; but if someone yells "fire" in a movie theatre and someone gets trampled to death, you can bet that the person who did the yelling has some explaining to do. When robbers go inside a bank and kill a bank teller, even though the getaway driver is parked outside, he is still charged with the murder.

In the post-9/11 world, an evil sect of the Muslim religion is trying to radicalize people in this country and around the globe to "jihad." What do you think people in this country are doing when they call for attacks on United States police officers? Especially when they tell you to question the police's authority, to resist lawful contact with police, and to disobey, run, talk back, attack, spit, or throw rocks at them.

We are radicalizing our own citizens against our very line of defense—the decent humanity tasked with protecting our way of life. If we put half the effort into supporting our country's way of life that we do into supporting protestor's rights and decriminalization issues, we could preserve and elevate our nation to the rule of law it once enjoyed. We, as individuals and as a society, must make a sincere attempt to work on racial tensions, rather than returning to the social divide of a century ago.

Here I will mention race. Of the two NYPD cops that were killed, one was Asian and the other was Latino. Both were good men with families; both were in the business of saving people and protecting the peace of a city that was attacked on 9/11. The person who killed them was mentally disturbed, a hardened convict with an extensive criminal record. Oh, yes, and he happened to be an African American.

Does the media report over and over again that a black man killed an Asian man and a Latino man? From the suspect's own tweets, he was going to "kill a couple of pigs." What do you think the media and this country's leaders would have said if the Asian and Latino officers had killed a black suspect? Yes, it is a rhetorical question and I think we all know the answer.

When these honorable men and women who wear a badge deserve our gratitude and respect, some politicians rush instead to a criminal's home and community to *console them*. Then some of our national leaders stay away from the controversy and remain silent. Who rushes to the home of the police officer to console his or her family? Actions really do speak louder than words.

The concept called leadership must be on duty 24/7, just like the cops.

Here is a bit of irony for you: When we wage war as a country, we always provide reparations to the war-torn nation with money and resources. We pump millions of dollars of foreign aid to countries to help rebuild or to fight disease, starvation, or rebelling against an oppressive regime. Then our Justice Department goes into a small, poor city like Ferguson, Missouri, conducts their investigation, and exonerates the accused officer, but in the same breath states that there is a pattern of racism and harassment in that town. What did they think the response was going to be? As I said earlier in this chapter, we saw this in New York after protestors were allowed to spew their hatred unopposed. Now the town of Ferguson is inflamed by the Justice Department's report. It's just like yelling "fire" in a movie theatre.

A few weeks after the Justice report, in March 2015, two police officers were standing on the street preparing for another night of demonstrations and were shot. These were not even local cops, but were assisting from another jurisdiction. One was shot in the back, the other in the face. Both will live, but with scars from an attack that was uncalled for and motivated not by the protestors, but by a coward. That city is in turmoil, and we, as a country, abandoned them. Finger pointing, political grandstanding, public criticism, and tweets were sent out by politicians, but they did not receive millions of dollars or federal assistance. Particularly since it was the federal government who said they identified the troublesome pattern in the American city called Ferguson.

If we, as a country, follow our customary practice of rebuilding other nations, feeding and educating their population, we should certainly be able to help rebuild our own communities and their police departments. I feel we MUST help, especially when such issues are screaming to our central beliefs as a nation of civil rights and the rule of law. Yet we hear only silence in the aftermath. We hear some public disdain for the ambush but no real support for that community. All that is said is that those bad cops need more training.

I was taught that when you criticize something or identify a problem, you just don't scream "fire" and walk away. You do something about it. You offer a few solutions. The government was quick to rally and meet with the nation's police chiefs to discuss training and other perceived issues with law enforcement. OK, that's great. But now, after the critique and discovery of—let's say the issues with the Ferguson Police Department, pump resources, experts, money, etc.—we need to help out that ravaged city. To abandon them after chastising them only sets them up for failure, resulting in open ambushes against innocent cops trying to keep the peace. If we are going to yell "fire," then we better be ready with water to put it out, instead of adding gasoline to the flames.

When the mayor of New York said about NYPD officers in the days prior to the assassination of two of their finest, "I have to tell my son to be careful when dealing with NYPD," or even when seemingly innocent statements are made like, "the police need to be retrained," they are only adding to the fever pitch that this country does not need from our leaders. Let's take a cue from Mr. Mandela. It takes moral courage to stand up for the right thing, especially when it is not popular or politically correct to do so. Maybe a statement by our elected leaders should go something like this instead:

"If I had a son, I would be an important part of his life, raise him to be a decent, law abiding young man that respects his neighbors, his nation's laws, police, and teachers, along with other people's property, and the city they live in. I would also tell him, 'If you find people tearing apart your community and walking the streets committing crime or chanting death to anyone, do something, say something, stand up and be heard. Only a coward would allow that kind of bullying to go on.' If I had a son or daughter motivated and inspired to serve in such a capacity in this country, I would support him or her in the tough job of being a cop, a teacher, or a soldier, and so should you. Don't judge until all the facts are in, hold all people accountable for their actions, no matter what side of the issue they are on. And remember, no one is above the law."

Maybe a politician or two, or a media outlet, could say something like that.

Another phrase that seemed to get some traction prior to these use-of-force situations capturing the media's attention was the "militarization of the police." Of course the public felt disgust at this idea. But remember that cops are being shot at when they pull over a car, as happened in Los Angeles on March 14, 2015, and being killed in their patrol cars while they take a lunch break as occurred in New York. They are being killed by terrorists while walking a beat as happened to the French police woman. A college campus officer was sitting in his patrol car when he was killed by the Boston terrorist bombers. And some police were simply finishing their shift and leaving the police barracks to go home in Pennsylvania when they were killed by a crazed gunman. All of these actions scream that we not only need to militarize our police, but that we better do it ASAP.

As both a patrol officer and a Special Agent, I always carried two guns on me, and I wore a vest every day. Believe me, I'd have driven a tank and carried a bazooka on patrol if they had issued me one. However, a realistic balance must be struck and constant policy reviews should be in place for the use of military-style equipment. If abuse occurs as a result of it being deployed, it will be addressed. If it saves the lives of the innocent public and cops, use it any chance you get.

No, the public should not and does not expect to have an M-1 Abrams tank roll up to their house on a barking dog call. But if there is a homicide suspect, high on drugs, who just shot up a bank, murdered his wife in a domestic dispute, or killed a bunch of kids on a college campus with an assault rifle and is now barricaded in a house, not only should a militarized police force respond, expect the tank.

Returning to civil protest, I support that right. I know the First Amendment is a wonderful thing, and this country has bent over backwards to defend that right, including sending our soldiers to war to do so. Even the burning of our county's flag is seen as a permissible form of protest. What people shouldn't be able to do is march in our streets and scream at the top of their lungs to KILL another group (in this case cops). This is where leadership should have stepped in and said no. Would you let your kids act like this? The New York mayor and the city's politicians abdicated their duty to end the protest right there. The problem was, it would have looked like they were interfering with the protestor's rights. They erred on the side of wanting to stay popular with the masses rather than protecting the true minority who were under attack: their city's police officers.

The First Amendment does not give the right to Americans to threaten other Americans with death. This is the exact same crap that is going on the Middle East. They are slaughtering themselves, their cities, and their people. We are better than that!

I can recall a Los Angeles Dodgers baseball game on April 25, 1976, when a pair of protestors wanted a chance to express their right to free speech during the day, in the middle of center field at Dodger Stadium. During the game, two protesters (a father and his young son), ran onto the field and tried to set fire to an American flag. The Dodgers were playing against the Cubs when Rick Monday, playing at the time for the Chicago Cubs, ran over and scooped up the flag to the roar of applause. He next gave the flag to Los Angeles Pitcher Doug Rau and the two flag burning protestors were arrested by the Police. When Rick Monday came up to bat in the next inning of the game, I remember he got a standing ovation from the crowd and on the big screen score board behind the left-field bleachers in the stadium flashed the message for the whole ball park and nationwide audience to see, "RICK MONDAY ... YOU MADE A GREAT PLAY..."

He reminded the public by later saying, "If you're going to burn the flag, don't do it around me. I've been to too many veterans' hospitals and seen too many broken bodies of guys who tried to protect it." Rick Monday was a member of the U.S. military, having served a commitment with the Marine Corps Reserve as part of his ROTC obligation after leaving Arizona State University. Years later, Rick Monday was presented with an American flag flown over Valley Forge National Historical Park in honor of the 1976 flag rescue and reminder to all on how a professional athlete should behave.

Rick Monday still has the flag he rescued from the protesters. He has been offered up to $1 million to sell it, but has declined all offers. At the September 2, 2008, Los Angeles Dodgers game, Rick Monday was presented with a Peace One Earth medallion by Patricia Kennedy, founder of the nonprofit organization Step Up 4 Vets, for his actions on April 25, 1976.

If this same event happened today, the protestors would probably be allowed to carry out their intentions, and it would all be aired on national TV; some of the professional athletes might even wear a T-shirt celebrating it … and a Major League Baseball player would probably have been arrested for interfering with their right to protest.

Some professional athletes today could use more of Rick Monday's type of courage and intellectual honesty. Frankly, we all could.

Let's consider the question of racial equality a little more. There seems to be a public outcry that there are not enough African American, Latino, or Asian officers. Society also seems to feel that local and federal political offices lack minority representation. This is another reality that this country needs to constructively address, rather than making a blanket accusation against law enforcement agencies. You will never have a community with an absolute perfect ratio of minority officers to the public it serves. Maybe it will be possible in one or two more generations from now, but not now. To infer that only Latino or black officers can police Latino or black communities is both ignorant and racist. The best hiring practices for recruitment, testing and selection are in place across this country, but, quite simply, the candidates are not. How to attract and retain cops, particularly in dangerous areas of our country, is a challenge and is debated nationwide. We must recognize that populations, demographics, and pay are varied, and that this is not the most popular line of work.

Federal and city governments cannot regulate where certain races of population are allowed to live, neither can law enforcement agencies. They do strive for a balanced and racially-diverse workforce. So too does the rest of government. That is always the goal. As we austerely test to get the best candidate for this job (police work), there must also be community support and ideas, rather than the "divide and conquer" approach. In April 2015, in Baltimore, another Ferguson-type unrest took place. There they have many African American officers in their ranks, as well as a mayor. Our country also has an Attorney General, and even a U.S. President who are African American. At what point does race just cloud an issue rather than point to the behavior of the individual? Now is the time to brainstorm and support a solution. It is NOT time for another race riot or a political grandstand.

Law enforcement agencies can't recruit, train, and make good cops out of thin air. There are hiring standards and rigorous psychological and physical exams; and the tests don't stop. They go on for your entire law enforcement career. As I went through my career, the tests came every day, at every call for service, at every arrest, and at every annual performance review (or "APR" as we used to call it). With each public contact or confrontation, with each appearance in the courts to testify in front of lawyers and judges, with every report we write, and every time we put a suspect in the hospital or use our handcuffs or guns, we are constantly under scrutiny. Add to this that the public is ultimately our customer. If anyone files a complaint, it typically gets investigated, as mandated by law. Sometimes it generates a more serious complaint and an Internal Affairs Investigation, or "IA" as it is commonly referred to.

The accusation of unlawful or objectionable action by a law enforcement officer is always taken seriously, and the accusation is enough to start the investigation process. That is something we as cops understand. It is our system, and it works. The complaint is investigated and the suspect in these cases (the cop) is put under a stress that few jobs subject their employees to. These complaints can be submitted by the public or from within the agency by fellow cops or management. So there are two "fronts" from which cops are constantly scrutinized on how they act and behave.

I was never really concerned about public or internal complaints since I knew how to do my job lawfully and successfully, and I took care to do my job professionally. Particularly when it came to the bad guys, I knew the rules of engagement. I wanted to be fair and passionate about doing the right thing, so I paid attention to the regulations and ethics of my profession.

Even so, I have been under a few IAs in my time as a cop. It will happen to everyone in the business if they are in it long enough. These investigations are not fun. When an Internal Affairs investigation is launched, the suspect (a police officer) is notified via a complaint letter that outlines the allegations. If the allegations weren't so serious, it would be laughable. Some accusations are absolutely preposterous in their very nature, but they have to be investigated since that is the system we work under and all swore an oath to be a part of. Cops can't hide behind the Fifth Amendment like criminals can. We are ordered, then compelled, to either make a statement or get fired for insubordination. What kind of job has a clause saying you must forfeit your right against self-incrimination? Police work does.

Let me digress for just a moment: Let's say, for argument's sake, I was a government employee who had mismanaged billions of dollars of taxpayer money, did not deliver a national project on time, and then lied to my boss. If I were held to the same standards as a police officer, not only would I have been fired, I would have been compelled to give a statement incriminating myself and suffering prosecution on top of that. Police are held to a higher standard, and I think executive levels of government should be too.

In my time as a law enforcement officer, I was accused of everything just short of murder and have had my Miranda rights read to me. (That was a really weird experience since I was the one who usually read these rights to real crooks.) In each instance, I was found innocent, and I was completely exonerated since the complaints were unfounded. I can say it made me appreciate even more the absolute privilege and power that the American police officer is entrusted with. We are subject to the same rule of law—and much more so than the public has to abide by. It has to be that way since we have the ability to incarcerate, detain, and search people and their homes and sometimes even take a human life in the performance of our duties.

The testing and training for law enforcement officers is constant in all these areas and more. Legal updates, medical updates, weapons training, seeing traumatic crime scenes, dealing with victims of horrific acts of violence, being a kind ear to an elderly patient who wandered away from home, dealing with the mentally ill, arresting criminals, emergency vehicle operations, hostage negotiations, and psychological techniques are just a few of the duties that make the average cop an attorney, social worker, doctor, caregiver, CEO, and gunfighter all rolled up into one.

Keep this in mind next time you encounter a member of the law enforcement. Also keep it in mind when you are sharing your views about law enforcement with your children or other young, impressionable people. Here are some common sense rules I would share with the public when dealing with police:

- Pull over when red lights and sirens are behind you. When you run, it is a sign of guilt, or what we call in police work, a clue.
- Don't damage property that is not your own.
- Don't ever throw rocks or bottles or spit on a cop.
- Treat all persons with respect and fairness (I know, seems pretty basic, but a lot people forgot this one).
- Cops are not your punching bags. We will NEVER take a punch so you can feel better.
- Cops are not karate experts or the Lone Ranger. If you arm yourself with a weapon, the cop will not stop to take time to discuss your troubled upbringing, racial biases, or your home life. The gun or knife will not be magically shot out of your hand. Comply with the order to drop the weapon.
- Cops don't shoot to get your attention; it is to stop you from being a threat. Sometimes stopping the threat results in killing the threat. No good cop wants to kill, but will do so if necessary.
- Adult supervision is truly a good thing. (An old partner of mine, Iggy, used to say this a lot and he was right.) Those with children need to practice it every day. It's not a cop's job or a teacher's job to raise your kids.
- At the end of the day, police can't control every situation. People aren't easily controlled when they are in a state of rage or agitation, or when they are high or drunk. The public is equally responsible in keeping the peace.

8

What It Takes to Wear
the Badge

"Courage is fear holding on a minute longer."

— GENERAL GEORGE S. PATTON

The experiences I have shared with you are unique to the profession of law enforcement, and most cops have been exposed to the situations I described in this book. In this job, we see a part of the society that few realize is actually part of the human experience, particularly as it relates to the justice system. When cops are put in a maelstrom and have seconds (if even that) to react and handle absolute chaos, they are vilified for making life-and-death decisions that only King Solomon could make after days of deliberations. You are either the hero or the goat.

I went through two police academies in my career. Contrary to what some think, I've had more training in my career than most get in a lifetime. My first academy was with the L.A. County Sheriff's Department, and my second police academy was with the

California Department of Justice. The constant chronic accusations that cops, particularly white cops, are trained to be or are already racist is absurd. I had 100 percent attendance in each of my academies, and I must have missed out on the secret class where the scene like the one in *Blazing Saddles* took place. There were a lot of cops from different ethnic and socioeconomic backgrounds; and yes, we did have minorities in our police academies. I know, because I was one of them.

Fast forward to 2012, when there were more than 50 BNE-led task forces in California in full operation. Their outstanding success in combatting crime throughout the state during the past 40 years is a book unto itself. However, the state's fragile economy and political will dictated a reorganization that eliminated BNE's participation in most of these task forces. Next came the unprecedented layoffs of Special Agents, along with demotions based on seniority. Local law enforcement screamed to the governor's office to keep BNE leadership in position, working narcotic cases, but the public and politicians were changing their attitudes towards policing and it was a losing proposition. This also happened to other law enforcement agencies across California and in most states.

In 2015, the California DOJ and other agencies are seeing some of these programs and personnel returning because of necessary adjustments and recognition of valuable missions that address violent crime, narcotic enforcement, and quality-of-life issues in our country. I am optimistic this ship will right itself. It looks like law enforcement and government leadership are trying to keep their eye on the ball, but both have to be constantly educated. This is the cyclical nature of law enforcement in an evolving society.

They just have to be reminded.

The average citizen usually comes in contact with law enforcement only when they are victimized, in need of help, or committing criminal acts. Rules for behavior are established in the various laws across this land. As for the narcotic plague, most get exposed to the drug culture by virtue of a "friend" offering them a taste of the poison. Most honest and reasonable people, I truly believe, really know it is a dangerous thing to do, and the ones that may have tried drugs recognized that it was not the type of life habit to form. They grew up and made the right choice. Those same leaders should talk to victims of crime and the general population about the harm that drugs, booze, and the career criminal present to our communities. Toss in a dialog about being a responsible parent or friend to someone in trouble, and help spread the word. This attitude must change or society will continue to pay the hefty price of a substandard quality of life and an erosion of civil rights that we should all enjoy equally, not selectively.

Logic demands we keep the anti-drug and law-enforcement efforts actionable and not tied to the circadian rhythms of society's moods.

I have seen this cycle over the past decades. We, as a society, can keep the crime and drug problem in check by keeping law enforcement efforts in place. But we need to balance these efforts with public awareness, education, prevention, and respect for each other. Also keep in mind the rule of law that law governs our nation. Integral to this is a respect for the cops tasked with protecting the public. This can be a success, but only if society and the police work together.

It takes a unique person to do the job of a law enforcement officer. You will see the usual knowledge and skill set advertised in the customary job bulletins, such as: must be over 21 years old, physically fit, have a college education, have good vision and hearing, and have a clean record. However, qualifications you will not see on the police officer job flier or application are: Must have a thick skin; the ability to handle every range of human emotion during an 8 hour shift; the ability to accept intense criticism from the department, the public, and the media; Must be able to be a role model to others; establish positive relationships with the community, particularly some communities that do not want you there; treat everyone equal regardless of what crime they committed and maintain a sense of fairness and compassion; possess the ability to think on your feet under stressful conditions, break up family fights, take kids away from parents who can't take care of them, and see kids and adults hurt or killed; a willingness to fight to the death with someone you never met till a minute ago; to comfort a victim of violent crime and pursue their attacker, or to help an elderly person cross the street; the ability to talk to a troubled kid and convince him or her to stay in school; and to look into the face of absolute terror and run towards it while others run away from it. You wouldn't see those qualifications listed and yet all of them are needed.

These are serious obligations for a serious job, and yet I would also add the requirement of having a life outside the job and a sense of humor. A certain amount of cynicism and trauma is going to happen; that is just the reality of the job. One way to keep it in check is to laugh and laugh often. It is truly is the best medicine. The duties of the job have to be balanced with family and friends to support the calling to be a cop. It is more than just another career.

Of course there are rogue officers, but they are ultimately dealt with. For every one of those tarnished badges, I could show you 100 cops who you would be proud to call your neighbor and friend.

Consider the following analogy of society and law enforcement's efforts in relation to bank robberies.

Back in the early 1800s and 1900s, bank robbery was the crime of choice. There is no need for a history lesson, but all of us need to be reminded of this. It is painfully simple.

As the Wild West days roared, bank robberies became the quickest way to make a lot of money. Our financial institutions, one would think, should have been guarded more diligently but initially they were not. We trusted our society to behave politely. That didn't happen. Bank robbers would storm into a bank, wield a gun, and have the employees hand over the money. Society got fed up and said, "Enough is enough." It took us a few years to figure this one out, but eventually guards were put at banks and locked drawers and safes were in place. The bandits realized this and started to use dynamite to blast into safes. Next, the safes were put in back rooms. Robbers brought more dynamite and more robbers to take over the bank. The banks reacted and made stronger safes and rooms called vaults.

The bandits knew the lawman's response was typically slow and only the town sheriff would show up, so they knew they could take over the bank with a gang of bandits. Next, the banks set up alarm systems to notify the local sheriff or marshal that a robbery was taking place. The bandits started to use more force and work more quickly. The vaults were now fortified. So some decided it was easier to approach a bank teller at a window and get just a few bucks but with less grief. No dynamite was needed to blow up safes or vaults; they just grabbed the money that was not as secure. Banks then responded with bulletproof glass in front of the tellers. Cameras were installed and record any robbery inside the bank. This gave us photos of the robber. Well, robbers figured that out and started to wear masks, ball caps, sunglasses, or other disguises.

Violence increased and bank robbers started killing innocent victims during the commission of the crime. Society decided to change its laws, making penalties stiffer. The driver of the getaway car used to be able to plead innocent since he did not pull the trigger, but only drove the bandits to the bank. But society said no. The driver now can be charged with murder should his co-conspirators kill someone inside the bank while committing the robbery. The boiling point was reached and society looked at its laws again.

Now to the present day. Yes, bank robberies still occur but nowhere near as frequently. When the robbers started to jump over the short counters at the teller windows, the banks made the bulletproof glass go all the way up to the ceiling. Then suspects thought maybe just grabbing a few money bags would be a quick scheme to make a clean get away. Today, moneybags have explosive dye packs in them, so if the suspect gets away, he has a rude awakening when he opens the bag and is covered in purple paint. Everyone will know he is either a bank robber or a man who enjoys bathing in grape juice.

Police now arrive within minutes of silent alarms; bank vaults and bank staff are prepared; armed guards are on the premises.

Sentencing for bank robbery is stiff. It is much harder today to rob a bank than it was in the last century.

Did we legalize bank robberies? Of course not. Did we become lenient towards those who would steal from us? The answer is no. The criminals (the behaviors) are held accountable.

We adapted to the criminal and made it harder for them to commit the robbery. Bank robberies continue to this day, but are not the crime wave they used to be. We as a society remained vigilant, keeping our eye on the ball.

The same should be true for the narcotic and career criminal offenders. Recidivism rates are alarming. A lot of criminals return to crime and addiction because that is all they know. There is no reason for legalizing drugs because time and time again, society demonstrates that its members are not capable of being responsible, law abiding, casual or recreational users when under the influence of cocaine, heroin, marijuana, PCP, meth, ecstasy, or any of the other popular yet dangerous drugs. We will never stop the drug scourge, just as we can't completely stop other crimes, but we can slow it down, keep it in check, and try to help those who want help.

Studies from the U.S. DOJ on crime and drug use show that over 75 percent of arrested criminals are drug users. Other studies have shown that high school drug testing can inhibit its use, and thus maybe save a graduating class or two from wasting their lives. I witnessed this in my law enforcement career. If we can get to our youth, send them the right message, and protect them from the lure of drugs, then they will not grow up to be addicts living off the welfare of family, the government, or federal prison.

It is now the year 2015. Let's not do the same thing over and over again by allowing drugs and crime to run rampant because we watered down laws or were so lenient that we just said, "Go ahead, buy all the drugs you want, behave irresponsibly because no one ever really gets hurt." Repeating the same legalization approach and softening our posture on crime, hoping for a different result, is the definition of insanity.

As I write this book, I remember the numerous police funerals I attended over the years. I personally know friends, coworkers, and fellow law enforcement officers that have died trying to protect our American way of life. Can you name 130 people in your line of work that die every year? California usually has the dubious distinction of leading the nation in this annual tragedy. I also reflect on the best times of a life in public service shared with incredibly brave and decent men and women who made a difference every day as they went out across the nation to do police work. It is a unique life changing career, with a lot of satisfaction, some heartache, and the ultimate test of how one person can make a difference. But, there is a human cost.

In early 2003, a classmate from my basic police academy was killed, shot by a crazed man waving a gun at his wife. My former classmate, David Powell, was an L.A. County deputy sheriff when he responded to the scene. He went up to the front door of the house and immediately came under fire and was killed.

Another partner of mine from BNE, Special Agent Patrick Dillon, was killed in the line of duty in 2007 as he attempted to protect us from the clandestine methamphetamine manufacturer. He never saw it coming; his killer ended up being the numerous exposures to the chemicals found at the labs he busted. As a direct result from the toxic environment he worked in, he contracted cancer and ultimately succumbed to it.

Lastly, another BNE Special Agent, Andre Tate, who was both my partner and good friend, suddenly and tragically died of natural causes. This occurred just one year before he was to retire. His day-in and day-out valor during our many harrowing nights chasing armed and dangerous criminals was a constant inspiration to me to be the best cop I could be. He spoke at my retirement in 2012 and we laughed, reminisced, and drank a toast to our brave partners who made the ultimate sacrifice. I now raise a glass and toast him, to thank him for protecting me during my career. As a side note, none of these courageous cops I mentioned made it to their 55th birthday.

I was fortunate to have shared some truly amazing and humbling times with an exceptional group of professionals. To be a part of something larger than yourself, serving the public in a way that makes our cities and our country a better place, to live a life of service for others, is without a doubt, the experience of a lifetime, regardless of the BS behind the badge.

While conducting marijuana eradication missions during the Ca. DOJ's C.A.M.P. (Campaign Against Marijuana Planting) season in 1987, I encountered this bobby trap while entering a "garden" (term for marijuana grow site). This is a 5x3 piece of plywood with 4" inch rusty nails protruding through the back side of the board. It was loosely covered with leaves and placed on the trail leading to the garden. Also, there was a trip wire (a thin metal cable) tied between two trees, a few feet in front of the trap. So, if one was not paying attention, you would trip and as you fell forward, impale yourself onto the nails. Lucky for me I saw this and avoided serious injury.

The marijuana garden. These plants stood nearly 5-6 feet tall and were hidden in one of the most scenic national forests in California. The C.A.M.P. season was in full bloom as BNE Special agents teamed up with local law enforcement in towns like Garberville, Willits, Whitethorn and Legget.

A clandestine laboratory located in a commercial warehouse district in Southern California. Present were all the chemicals, glassware, heating mantles and laboratory apparatus needed to manufacture multi-pound quantities of methamphetamine. I had to wear protective clothing with boots and gloves in order to avoid being contaminated while processing this crime scene.

Weapons of choice for the Mexican drug cartels. During a "routine" search warrant in Los Angeles while investigating a heroin trafficking organization, these weapons were found in the home. The AK-47 (fully automatic) was propped in the corner next to the front door. The .38 Super, a semi-automatic pistol was on the coffee table as we secured the residence. Both weapons were loaded with a round in the chamber, ready to go.

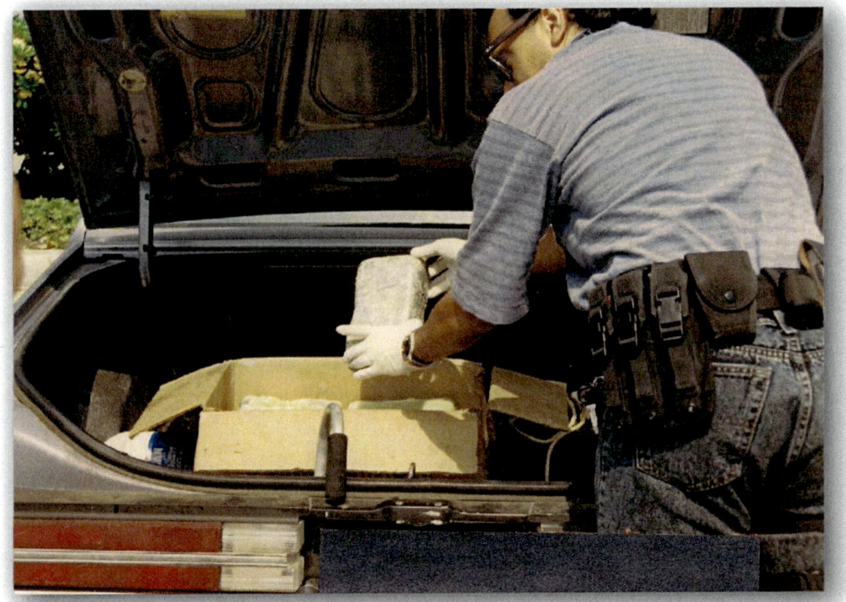

Multiple kilograms of cocaine, seized after a "buy / bust" operation by LA BNE Special Agents. I am holding up a rectangular object that is a typical kilo (1000 grams) of cocaine.

BNE Special Agents conducting entry training at Camp Pendleton, San Diego. This facility is called the M.O.U.T. (Military Operations in Urban Terrain) and allows law enforcement to realistically train in a live fire environment while honing their room clearing tactics. From left to right; me (breacher), then Bill, Andy, Dwayne and Doug.

Photo of Ca. DOJ Special Agent badge.

Acknowledgements

You have to have a sense of "on duty" and "off duty" or go crazy seeing the things that one runs across in this line of work. My fellow cops and co-workers make this job a career to enjoy and cannot be done without them. Also there is the obvious seriousness that is the very nature of police work. Whether you are a local, state, federal, or tribal cop, I know you can relate to this experience. To the newer police generation: learn the history of our profession and pay attention to policing and politics. They go hand in hand. History tends to repeat itself, and if you live through it, you can warn society to stay on track and keep its eye on the ball.

Every cop has a book they can write, and I draw from my times in working with the most fascinating people I have ever met. From my time at the police department to being a State Special Agent, I was able to cross that finish line and retire where a lot my friends did not. I could fill up pages acknowledging all those good cops, great professional staff, supervisors, and leaders that were part of my journey. Add to that all the friends and family who supported me throughout the years, including a fireman or two. I would truly not be here if it wasn't for each and every one of them.

I still pay my respects at law enforcement funerals every year. That is the ultimate reminder of what we do for our nation. I will continue to attend them for as long as I can and for many reasons, but primarily to support the family and the agency that lost a human being who cared enough to wear the badge with honor.

I could not have written this book without the keen instinct from my patriot, Sarah "#4". I also had many a discussion with John "Mr. Torta", Al "Dr. Albert", and Blaine "the County Mountie" (they know who they are), to keep my perspective. Thank you all for the honest feedback and for being part of my life as I lived through what Disneyland used to call an "E" ticket ride. A heartfelt thank you to my editor, Amy Paul of P2 Editorial Services, whose sharp eye helped smooth out the rough edges of my ideas and kept me focused on my intended concepts rather than the tangential topics that would occasionally launch me into orbit. Amy, you are a patient lady and very wise.

Finally, to all the cops still out there trying to make a difference, stay safe.

i. John M. Volant, *Dying from the Job: The Mortality Risk for Police Officers* (Elmira, Ore.: Law Enforcement Wellness Association, 1996).

ii. According to the Officer Down Memorial Page (ODMP) (https://www.odmp.org/), the domestic disturbance call involved reports of an emotionally disturbed man attempting to break into his parents' home. Deputy Lee, a solo patrol officer, responded to the call. He contacted the reported irate family member and was immediately involved in a violent struggle with the suspect, The suspect knocked out Deputy Lee, took away his baton, and beat him with his own nightstick. Deputy Lee suffered severe head injuries. Luckily backup arrived within minutes. Deputy Lee's backup officer arrived on the scene and found him unconscious. The suspect then began to approach the backup officer with the baton. The suspect refused to drop the baton and was shot and killed. Deputy Lee was transported to Desert Regional Medical Center where he succumbed to his injuries and died approximately two hours later. Deputy Lee had been a member of the Riverside County Sheriff's Department for 22 years.

iii. The Andean Information Network (http://ain-bolivia.org/) cites that the coca leaf was cultivated and distributed throughout the central and northern Andean Ridge. Coca, the sacred leaf or "hoja divina," has been used within the Andean society since approximately 3000 BC. During the Incan empire, the plant was considered sacred, and consumption of the coca leaf was reserved for the upper classes.

iv. Major General Perry M. Smith, USAF retired, is a graduate of the U.S. Military Academy at West Point, and earned a PhD in International Relations from Columbia University. An internationally known speaker and media commentator, he has conducted seminars on leadership, strategic planning, and ethics for hundreds of organizations, including Harvard's Kennedy School and Microsoft.

v. **Department of Justice. (March 3, 2004)** Attorney General John Ashcroft . . . announced that Muhamed Abid Afridi and Ilyas Ali pled guilty today in federal court in San Diego to the felony charges of conspiracy to provide material support to terrorists and conspiracy to distribute heroin and hashish. . . . Ashcroft stated, "Terrorism and drug trafficking often thrive in the same conditions, support each other, and feed off each other. These guilty pleas are reminders that the Al Qaeda terrorist network continues to use any and all illicit means to finance, plan and perpetrate their acts of violence. While this case highlights the ongoing, transnational threat of terrorism and drug trafficking, it also shows that law enforcement agencies around the world are focused and cooperating in combating terrorist and drug trafficking activity. Because of the actions taken in this investigation, America is safer and our citizens are more secure." . . . Both defendants admitted that they conspired to distribute approximately five metric tons of hashish and 600 kilograms of heroin originating in Pakistan to undercover United States law enforcement officers. Additionally, the defendants admitted that they conspired to receive, as partial payment for the drugs, four

"Stinger" anti-aircraft missiles which they intended to then sell to the Taliban, an organization they knew at the time to be the same as Al-Qaeda. [Press release] Retrieved from http://www.justice.gov/archive/opa/pr/2004/March/04_ag_136.htm

vi. According to the ODMP, the line-of-duty deaths in 2014 totaled 127, with the following breakdown:
9/11 related illness: 1
Assault: 2
Automobile accident: 26
Drowned: 2
Duty-related illness: 3
Fire: 1
Gunfire: 47
Gunfire (Accidental): 2
Heart attack: 19
Motorcycle accident: 4
Struck by vehicle: 5
Vehicle pursuit: 5
Vehicular assault: 10
Retrieved from: https://www.odmp.org/search/year?year=2014

vii. The National Law Enforcement Officers Memorial Fund (http://www.nleomf.com/) notes that, on average, one law enforcement officer is killed in the line of duty somewhere in the United States every 58 hours. Since the first known line-of-duty death in 1791, more than 20,000 U.S. law enforcement officers have made the ultimate sacrifice.

viii. The Office of the Governor of the State of Pennsylvania (09/13/2014). Governor Tom Corbett Releases Statement on Shooting of Pennsylvania State Police Trooper [Press release]. Retrieved from http://www.pa.gov/Pages/NewsDetails.aspx?agency=pagovnews&item=16018#.VTexcyHBzGc.

ix. KARACHI, Pakistan (www.dailymail.co.uk) — [Gulzar Ahmed] recalled how days before his brother's [Didar Ahmed] death, they had talked about the rising dangers of police work as officers increasingly come under attack by criminal gangs and militants from the Pakistani Taliban. "He was sitting here and told me: 'The situation in the city is deteriorating so if something happens to me, you take care of my kids and family,'" Gulzar said. Ahmed was one of 44 police officers killed during the first two months of the year in Pakistan's largest city, a particularly violent start to the year for the police. The force was already reeling from 166 officers killed last year — roughly one every other day and a four-fold increase from just five years earlier. (Retrieved from http://www.dailymail.co.uk/wires/ap/article-2579823/Police-attack-Pakistans-largest-city.html)

About the Author

Mr. Solano started his career as a city Police Officer then joined the California Department of Justice as a Special Agent where he worked for 25 years. During his three decade career he worked undercover and conducted major criminal investigations. As a Special Agent he also trained other law enforcement personnel in a variety of skills needed to conduct such casework. He was Special Agent of the year in 1995, then promoted thru the ranks, ultimately achieving the position of Special Agent in Charge. As the Special Agent in Charge of a statewide Ca. DOJ Division, he received the Ca. Attorney General's award for Excellence in Management. He successfully led many specialized units, bureaus and divisions tasked with a variety of investigative missions. Upon retirement from the Ca. DOJ, he continues to provide expertise and management services to the law enforcement profession.

42765512R00093

Made in the USA
San Bernardino, CA
08 December 2016